Education in the UK

Editor: Danielle Lobban

Volume 423

First published by Independence Educational Publishers

The Studio, High Green

Great Shelford

Cambridge CB22 5EG

England

© Independence 2023

ISBN-13: 978 1 86168 883 5

Printed in Great Britain

Zenith Print Group

Acknowledgements

The publisher is grateful for permission to reproduce the material in this book. While every care has been taken to trace and acknowledge copyright, the publisher tenders its apology for any accidental infringement or where copyright has proved untraceable. The publisher would be pleased to come to a suitable arrangement in any such case with the rightful owner.

The material reproduced in **issues** books is provided as an educational resource only. The views, opinions and information contained within reprinted material in **issues** books do not necessarily represent those of Independence Educational Publishers and its employees.

Images

Cover image courtesy of iStock. All other images courtesy of Freepik, Pixabay and Unsplash.

Additional acknowledgements

With thanks to the Independence team: Shelley Baldry, Tracy Biram, Klaudia Sommer and Jackie Staines.

Danielle Lobban

Cambridge, May 2023

Contents

Chapter 1: Education Today

Chapter 2: Issues in Education

Introduction

Education in the UK is Volume 423 in the **issues** series. The aim of the series is to offer current, diverse information about important issues in our world, from a UK perspective.

About Education in the UK

Education in the UK today is facing increasing challenges. Ever-decreasing budgets, a narrowing curriculum and the lingering effect of the pandemic are just a few of the contributing factors putting pressure on schools, colleges, teaching staff and students alike. This book looks at the impact of those issues as well as the rising trend in elective home-schooling, proposals to make maths study compulsory up to the age of 18 and changes to starting age.

Our sources

Titles in the **issues** series are designed to function as educational resource books, providing a balanced overview of a specific subject.

The information in our books is comprised of facts, articles and opinions from many different sources, including:

- Newspaper reports and opinion pieces
- Website factsheets
- Magazine and journal articles
- Statistics and surveys
- Government reports
- Literature from special interest groups.

A note on critical evaluation

Because the information reprinted here is from a number of different sources, readers should bear in mind the origin of the text and whether the source is likely to have a particular bias when presenting information (or when conducting their research). It is hoped that, as you read about the many aspects of the issues explored in this book, you will critically evaluate the information presented.

It is important that you decide whether you are being presented with facts or opinions. Does the writer give a biased or unbiased report? If an opinion is being expressed, do you agree with the writer? Is there potential bias to the 'facts' or statistics behind an article?

Activities

Throughout this book, you will find a selection of assignments and activities designed to help you engage with the articles you have been reading and to explore your own opinions. Some tasks will take longer than others and there is a mixture of design, writing and research-based activities that you can complete alone or in a group.

Further research

At the end of each article we have listed its source and a website that you can visit if you would like to conduct your own research. Please remember to critically evaluate any sources that you consult and consider whether the information you are viewing is accurate and unbiased.

Issues Online

The **issues** series of books is complemented by our online resource, issuesonline.co.uk

On the Issues Online website you will find a wealth of information, covering over 70 topics, to support the PSHE and RSE curriculum.

Why Issues Online?

Researching a topic? Issues Online is the best place to start for...

Librarians

Issues Online is an essential tool for librarians: feel confident you are signposting safe, reliable, user-friendly online resources to students and teaching staff alike. We provide multi-user concurrent access, so no waiting around for another student to finish with a resource. Issues Online also provides FREE downloadable posters for your shelf/wall/table displays.

Teachers

Issues Online is an ideal resource for lesson planning, inspiring lively debate in class and setting lessons and homework tasks.

Our accessible, engaging content helps deepen students' knowledge, promotes critical thinking and develops independent learning skills.

Issues Online saves precious preparation time. We wade through the wealth of material on the internet to filter the best quality, most relevant and up-to-date information you need to start exploring a topic.

Our carefully selected, balanced content presents an overview and insight into each topic from a variety of sources and viewpoints.

Students

Issues Online is designed to support your studies in a broad range of topics, particularly social issues relevant to young people today.

Thousands of articles, statistics and infographs instantly available to help you with research and assignments.

With 24/7 access using the powerful Algolia search system, you can find relevant information quickly, easily and safely anytime from your laptop, tablet or smartphone, in class or at home.

Visit issuesonline.co.uk to find out more!

issues online
resources for schools, colleges & libraries

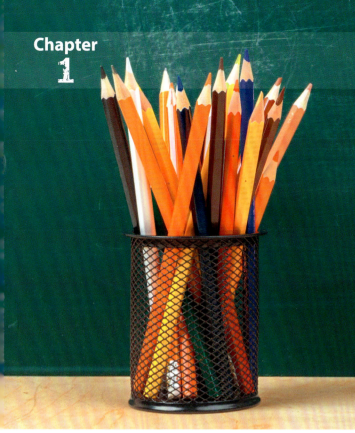

Education Today

Different types of schools in UK

The United Kingdom has different types of schools to deliver education at distinct levels. Here is a glimpse of different types of schools in the UK.

State-funded Schools

State-funded schools follow the National Curriculum*, with main subjects including English, math and science. State schools are reviewed by the Office for Standards in Education, Child Services and Skills (Ofsted) every three years.

*The National Curriculum is a set of subjects and standards used by primary and secondary schools.

Independent Schools

Independent schools are funded by student fees and interest earned on school funding/investments. They set their own curriculum

Home Schooling

Children aged 4-16 are schooled at home, taught by either their parents or tutors.

Special Schools

Special schools with students of the age 11 years and older can specialize in the following areas: communication and interaction, cognition and learning, behaviour, emotional and social development and sensory and physical needs

Faith Schools

Faith schools are associated with a particular religion. Faith schools follow the national curriculum except for religious studies, where they can teach about their own religion without any set curriculum. The admissions criterion varies.

Free Schools

Free schools are funded by the government but aren't run by the local council. Free schools are run on a not-for-profit basis and can be set up by groups like charities, Universities, independent schools, community and faith groups, teachers, parents, or businesses. Free schools can set their own conditions and school terms.

Types of free school:

- **University technical colleges:** University technical colleges specialise in subjects like engineering, IT, construction and business skills. The curriculum is designed by the university and employers, who also offer students the work and internship experience.

- **Studio schools:** Studio schools are small schools, usually with around 300 students, delivering mainstream qualifications through project-based learning, i.e. working in realistic situations as well as learning academic subjects. Students at Studio schools work with local employers and a personal coach, and conform to a curriculum planned to give them the skills and qualifications they require at work, or to take up further education.

Academies

Academies are publicly funded independent schools. They're run by an academy trust which employs the staff. Academies can set their own terms. Academies have sponsors such as commercial enterprises, universities, other schools, faith groups or voluntary groups.

City Technology Colleges

City technology colleges are independent schools in urban areas owned and funded by companies as well as central government. They are free to attend and lay major focus on technological and practical skills.

State Boarding Schools

State boarding schools offer free education, but charge fees for boarding. Some state boarding schools are run by local councils, and some are run by academies or free schools.

www.ukeducation.info

What is an academy and what are the benefits?

A blogpost from The Education Hub.

We want every school in the country to be part of a family of schools in a strong multi academy trust. But what are academies and what are the benefits of this plan?

The academies programme gives individual schools greater freedoms compared to local authority control. Being an academy gives schools the power to decide on the best curriculum for their pupils, determine how they spend their budgets, and much more.

What is an academy?

Academies are state-funded schools but they're independent from local authorities meaning they aren't run by councils. They can decide on their own curriculums, term dates, school hours and much more.

They're still funded by the government but they get to decide how they spend their money, from how much they pay teachers to how much they spend on classroom equipment.

Over half of pupils are already educated in academies and there are three types:

- Converters – formerly council-run schools that chose to become academies;

- Sponsored – previously under-performing council-run schools in need of support, and/or judged 'Inadequate' by Ofsted, where the law requires them to become academies; or

- Free schools – brand new schools established to meet a need for good school places in area.

Primary, secondary, middle, all-through, 16-19, alternative provision and special schools can all be academies.

What are multi academy trusts?

Multi academy trusts are charities that have responsibility for running a number of academies. They cannot, as charities, be run for financial profit and any surplus must be reinvested in the trust.

By working in partnership with each other, the schools within a trust can share staff, curriculum expertise and effective teaching practices, and work together to deliver the best outcomes for pupils.

While other types of school partnerships can be effective, the key difference with academy trusts is that there is shared accountability for standards across the trust; all schools within the trust support each other and the trust is accountable for them all.

Why is the government's focus now on supporting schools to join strong trusts?

Joining a multi academy trust remains a positive choice for schools. They enable the strongest leaders to take responsibility for supporting more schools, develop great teachers and allow schools to focus on what really matters – teaching, learning and a curriculum that is based on what works.

Every year, hundreds of schools choose to convert and benefit from the freedom that academy status can provide, at a timescale that suits them best.

As we build back better from the pandemic, multi-academy trusts have the capacity to provide the best training and evidence-based curriculum support for already great teachers, freeing them to focus on what they do best – teaching.

If they have all this freedom, how are they accountable?

This freedom does not mean academies are not regulated. The department's National and Regional Schools Commissioners and their teams, together with the Education and Skills Funding Agency, provide robust educational and financial oversight of all academy trusts.

Individual academies are still subject to Ofsted inspections and ratings in exactly the same way as council-run schools.

In fact, academies are subject to greater accountability than council-run schools because of increased financial regulation.

What happens if an academy fails? Can they be transferred back to local authorities?

If an academy is failing to meet the required standards, the current system allows the department to take swift action, including transferring the academy to a more suitable trust where necessary. But we don't believe transferring a school back into the control of a local authority is the best way to bring about improvement.

14 October 2021

What is a free school? Everything you need to know

All children in England between the ages of 5 and 16 are entitled to a free place at a state school.

All state schools receive funding through their local authority or directly from the government.

But there are different types of state school – these include free schools, which account for a significant number of the new schools being built and opened around the country.

Here we answer your questions on free schools.

What is a free school?

Free schools are a type of academy - schools that are run by charities rather than the local authority (council) and cannot be run for financial profit.

They are funded by central government and have a range of freedoms including the freedom to teach in an innovative way, whether that is focusing on STEM subjects or taking a different approach to learning.

Over 600 free schools are open across England. They include primary, secondary, all-through, and standalone sixth forms, as well as schools specifically for children with special educational needs or disabilities (SEND) or pupils who, because of illness of otherwise, would not receive a suitable education in mainstream settings (alternative provision).

The free school programme has delivered hundreds of new schools and provided thousands of good school places across the country.

86% of all free schools with inspection reports published by the end of April 2022 are rated 'Good' or 'Outstanding'.

What's the difference between a free school and academy?

Legally, free schools are academies. They are independent from local authorities (councils) and funded directly by the department. As with academies, free schools enjoy a range of freedoms including setting their own pay and conditions; greater control over their budget; freedom from following the national curriculum; and the freedom to change the length of school days.

The main difference is that free schools are newly set up schools whereas many academies as converters that were previously council run schools.

Who can attend a free school?

Anyone can attend a free school. Free schools are free to attend and must have admission arrangements that are clear and fair.

How can a free school be established?

Anybody can apply to set up a free school if they have the necessary capacity and capability.

Applications go through a rigorous assessment and must demonstrate how the proposal will meet key criteria, such as a clear need for the places the school will create, and how the school will be financially viable whilst offering a broad and balanced curriculum.

10 June 2022

Sunak outlines maths to 18 'ambition'… but not before 2025

Labour says 'reheated' pledge is 'empty without more maths teachers'.

By Freddie Whittaker

Rishi Sunak will set an 'ambition' for all school pupils to study 'some form of maths' until the age of 18.

But the prime minister will only commit to starting work to introduce the new policy in this Parliament.

He will acknowledge in a speech tomorrow that the proposed reform would not be achieved during the course of this Parliament – which will come to an end in 2024 at the latest.

The government also 'does not envisage' making maths A-Level compulsory for all students, Downing Street has said.

Ministers are 'exploring existing routes', such as the core maths qualification and T-levels, as well as 'more innovative' choices, Number 10 said this evening.

But there are no details about how more maths teachers would be recruited. Government has failed to recruit the required number of maths teachers since at least 2012, Labour analysis shows.

'Empty pledge without more maths teachers'

Shadow education secretary Bridget Phillipson said the prime minister 'needs to show his working'.

'He cannot deliver this reheated, empty pledge without more maths teachers, yet the government has missed their target for new maths teachers year after year, with existing teachers leaving in their droves.'

Sunak pledged during the first Conservative leadership campaign this summer to introduce a 'British baccalaureate', which he said would also involve compulsory English study in sixth form.

However, his government has focused on maths since taking office in October.

In a speech setting out his priorities for the year ahead, Sunak will say the ambition is 'personal for me'.

He will say 'every opportunity I've had in life began with the education I was so fortunate to receive'. He attended prep school and then the private Winchester College, whose fees for boarders currently top £45,000 a year.

'And it's the single most important reason why I came into politics: to give every child the highest possible standard of education.'

Ambition won't be delivered before 2025

He will pay tribute to the 'reforms we've introduced since 2010, and the hard work of so many excellent teachers, we've made incredible progress'.

'With the right plan – the right commitment to excellence – I see no reason why we cannot rival the best education systems in the world.'

The prime minister is expected to acknowledge the reforms won't be easy, with Downing Street tonight admitting there are 'practical challenges involved'.

Sunak is committing to starting the work to introduce maths to 18 in this Parliament, but not finishing it until the next.

The announcement will likely prompt scepticism about whether it will ever be realised, with the Conservatives mired in the polls.

Maths remains the most popular group of subjects at A-level, with just shy of 90,000 entries this summer.

On top of that, the roughly 145,000 pupils who don't get a grade 4 or above at GCSE continue to study the subject post-16 until they pass, while around 12,000 take a core maths qualification.

But the government said only around half of 16 to 19-year-olds study any maths at all, warning the problem is 'particularly acute for disadvantaged pupils'.

Downing Street also said the 'majority' of OECD countries, including Australia, Canada, France, Germany, Finland, Japan, Norway and the USA, require some form of maths study to 18.

Ministers already can't recruit enough maths teachers

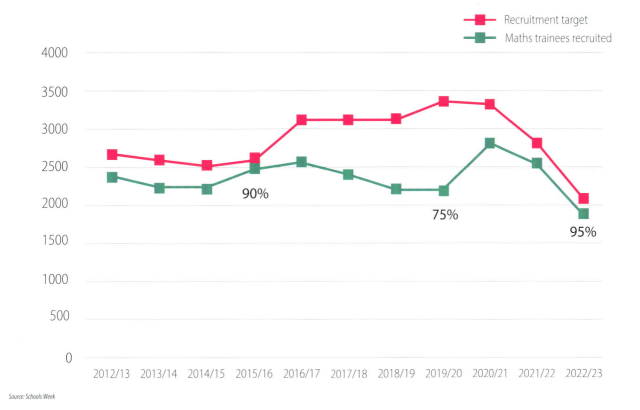

Source: Schools Week

Sunak will say that 'one of the biggest changes in mindset we need in education today is to reimagine our approach to numeracy.'

'Right now, just half of all 16–19-year-olds study any maths at all. Yet in a world where data is everywhere and statistics underpin every job, our children's jobs will require more analytical skills than ever before.

'And letting our children out into the world without those skills, is letting our children down'.

'Show us the evidence', says union boss

Geoff Barton, general secretary of the ASCL school leaders' union, said it was 'important that the government sets out the evidence for extending maths for all students to the age of 18 before embarking upon a significant change affecting future generations'.

'It may improve employability and the ability to cope with modern life, as the prime minister suggests, but it is important that this is based on solid research and is not a pet project.

'We would also want to hear how such a policy would avoid exacerbating the already-chronic national shortage of maths teachers.'

The idea of compulsory maths to 18 has been floated before.

In 2011, a report for the Conservative Party by mathematician and TV presenter Carol Vorderman recommended all pupils should study maths to 18. But the recommendation was never followed.

In 2017, a further report on the feasibility of maths to 18 was commissioned by the government.

'Don't make maths a political football' says review author

In the document, Sir Adrian Smith concluded that there was a 'strong case for higher uptake of 16-18 mathematics', and said the government should 'set an ambition for 16-18 mathematics to become universal in 10 years'.

But he said there was 'not a case at this stage, however, for making it compulsory'.

'The appropriate range of pathways is not available universally, teacher supply challenges are significant and it is unclear when sufficient specialist capacity will be in place for universal mathematics to become a realistic proposition.'

Smith said today that the country needed to 'upgrade the post-16 approach as part of wider reform at secondary and post-16'.

'It is time for a baccalaureate style system that will give a broader education than the exceptionally narrow A-levels.'

He added that 'radical reform of the education system will not be easy and will take time but we need to get started now and build a cross party approach with support from teachers, students, parents and employers'.

'This matters too much to be a political football that could be punctured by the ebb and flow of politics.'

3 January 2023

Latest trends in further education and sixth form spending in England

Updated analysis of trends in further education and sixth form spending per pupil and upcoming resource challenges facing colleges and sixth forms.

By Luke Sibieta and Imran Tahir

Further education colleges and sixth forms saw some of the largest cuts in spending in the decade up to 2020. Since then, the government has increased funding for colleges and sixth forms. It has also emphasised the role of technical education in the levelling-up agenda and as part of efforts to improve productivity. The sector now faces a range of significant challenges. First, the number of 16- and 17-year-olds is rising rapidly as a result of a population boom moving through the education system. Second, the impact of the pandemic remains significant, with changes in young people's education decisions and the effects of lost learning. Third, just like everyone, colleges and sixth forms are facing rising costs as a result of rising levels of inflation. In this comment, we outline what is happening to student numbers and the challenges this creates for the sector. We also update our analysis of trends in spending per student and likely future trends in light of current economic forecasts.

Rising numbers of young people in full-time education

There has been a long-run rise in the number of young people in full-time education (see Figure 1). Since the mid 1980s, the proportion of 16- and 17-year-olds in full-time education has more than doubled from around 40% to 84%. This has been accompanied by a decline in the share of this age group in part-time education or training (which includes apprenticeships) and full-time employment.

Part-time education and employment seem to have fallen especially sharply due to the pandemic: full-time employment fell by 5% between 2019 and 2020 while part-time education or training fell by 12% in the same period. Although there has been a slight recovery in part-time education, full-time employment among 16- and 17-year-olds continues to decline. By the end of 2021, only 9% of 16- and 17-year-olds were in part-time education or training and 2% were in full-time employment, which is the lowest level ever recorded.

Figure 1. Participation in education and employment of 16- and 17-year-olds in England

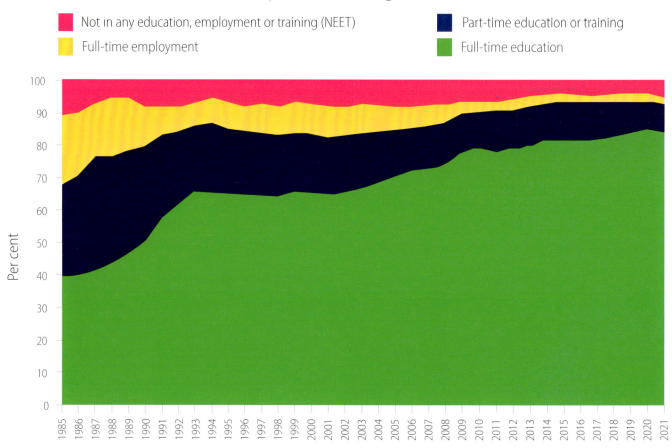

Source: Department for Education, 'Participation in education, training and employment: 2021' and 'Participation on education, training and employment age 16 to 18.'

Figure 2. Qualifications by 16- and 17-year-olds in England 2021

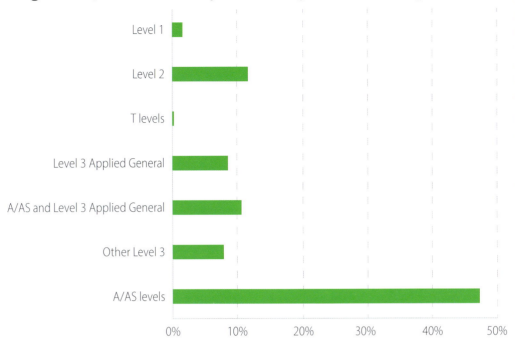

Qualification	
Level 1	
Level 2	
T levels	
Level 3 Applied General	
A/AS and Level 3 Applied General	
Other Level 3	
A/AS levels	

(Horizontal axis: 0% to 50%)

Source: Department for Education, 'Participation institution and qualification data'.

By the end of 2021, 5% of 16- and 17-year-olds (or around 65,000 young people) were not in education, employment or training (NEET), which represents an increase of almost 15,000 on the previous year. This means that the NEET rate among 16- and 17-year-olds is at its highest level since 2013. Whilst this is still well below the 7–8% seen for most of the 2000s, any increase in the NEET rate for young people is particularly worrying given the potentially detrimental long-run consequences of inactivity for young people.

It is also important to understand the sort of qualifications young people study for (see Figure 2). The majority of young people who continue in education study A levels: 58% of all 16- and 17-year-olds study either solely A levels or a combination of A levels and other qualifications. Most of these students will be undertaking these A levels in school sixth forms or sixth-form colleges.

Under the 16 to 19 funding formula, most of these study programmes attract the national base rate of funding. Between 2013–14 and 2019–20, the national base rate was frozen at £4,000 in cash terms, which means that its real value was eroded by 9%. While it is difficult to make comparisons prior to 2013–14 since funding was calculated on a different basis, we know that policy was equivalent to a cash-terms freeze from 2010–11 to 2013–14. As a result, the real-terms value of funding for most study programmes is likely to have declined by a lot more than 9% over the last decade.

The base rate was increased to £4,188 in 2020–21 and then to £4,542 for 2022–23 (all figures in cash terms). This reflects a policy commitment to fund an extra 40 hours of teaching time for most full-time programmes and T levels, as well as expected inflationary pressures and consolidating the teachers' pay grant into the main settlement (funding for the cost of higher employer pension contributions remains separate).

Although A levels are the most common qualification route, almost 20% of this age group study at least one Applied General Qualification (such as BTECs or Technical Certificates).

These are mostly undertaken in further education colleges. In addition to the national base rate of funding, many of these technical qualifications receive extra funding for being more complicated or costly to deliver.

Earlier this year, the first cohort of T-level students – who began their courses in 2020 – received their grades, but only 0.4% of all 16- and 17-year-olds studied these qualifications in 2021 (the most recent year for which we have data). T levels receive funding ranging from £9,446 to £13,068 for a two-year programme of study, depending on the number of planned hours of teaching.

Over time, as more young people take T levels, the government intends to withdraw funding from other overlapping qualifications (such as BTECs). In October 2022, the government published the final list of qualifications that will have their funding withdrawn from August 2024, which amounts to just over 100 qualifications. This includes a range of qualifications, including BTECs and City and Guilds qualifications, in subject areas that overlap with T levels that have been rolled out.

The school-age population rose rapidly over the 2010s. This population boom is now passing into sixth forms and colleges. Between 2019 and 2022, the number of 16- and 17-year-olds in England grew by 9% or an additional 110,000 young people. This age group is projected to continue growing during this decade (see Figure 3). The Office for National Statistics (ONS) projects that the total number of 16- and 17-year-olds in England will grow by a further 61/2% or 90,000 between 2022 and 2024. This would make for a

Figure 3. The projected number of 16- and 17-years-olds in England

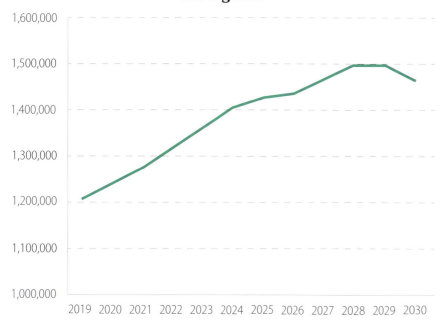

Source: Office for National Statistics, 'National population projections by single year of age'.

17% rise between 2019 and 2024 – or an extra 200,000 young people. Given current levels of participation, this would equate to over 160,000 extra students. As a result, schools and colleges will have to manage their budgets to educate a far larger number of students.

Beyond 2024, the number of 16- and 17-year-olds is set to continue rising until it peaks at around 1.5 million towards the end of this decade. This includes a further 2% rise between 2024 and 2026. This will make it more difficult to deliver any cuts to spending on colleges and sixth forms between 2024–25 and 2026–27 (years beyond those covered by the 2021 Spending Review).

How has spending per student changed over time?

Figure 4 illustrates spending per student aged 16–18 in school sixth forms, further education (FE) colleges and sixth-form colleges in each academic year from 2013–14 onwards. In this graph and the remaining analysis, we consider funding allocated per student aged 16–18, as opposed to actual amounts of spending on students, which could be higher or lower depending on how schools and colleges allocate funding for different stages of education.

In each year, spending per student aged 16–18 is noticeably higher in FE colleges. In the academic year 2021–22, FE colleges spent roughly £6,800 per pupil, compared with £5,300 in school sixth forms and £5,100 in sixth-form colleges. This is because students in FE colleges are more likely to study vocational qualifications and are more likely to come from deprived backgrounds, both of which attract higher levels of funding.

The pace of real-terms cuts between 2013–14 and 2019–20 was similar across school sixth forms and sixth-form colleges, with real-terms cuts of 16–17% since 2013–14. The cuts to FE colleges have been smaller at 8% between 2013–14 and 2019–20. This reflects the fact that FE colleges have gained more from new funding streams aimed at vocational qualifications.

The government has sought to reverse the decline in further education spending by allocating £2.3 billion in additional funding to colleges and sixth forms in 2024–25 compared with 2019–20. However, due to the rapid rise in student numbers, this additional spending only returns spending per student in 2021–22 back to 2018–19 levels, leaving in place much of the cuts in spending per student seen over the previous decade.

Whilst the figures show an apparent cut in spending per pupil in 2020–21, this is entirely driven by the volatility of the GDP deflator and inflation more generally during the pandemic. As a result, changes involving 2020–21 as a start or end year are unlikely to be reliable.

In Figure 5, we look at longer-term trends in spending per student and projected spending per student through to 2024–25 based on current spending plans and inflation forecasts. To do so, we must combine FE and sixth-form colleges, which we refer to as 16– 18 colleges, and track spending by financial year instead of academic year.

Over the 2000s, spending per student in colleges increased from around £5,100 per student to reach £7,500 per student in 2010–11, a real-terms increase of nearly 50% or 4% per year. Spending per student in school sixth forms increased from £6,500 in 2002– 03 (the earliest data point we have) to roughly £7,200 per student in 2010–11, a total increase of £700 or 11%. The faster growth amongst colleges meant that

Figure 4. Spending per student in further education colleges (16−18), sixth-form colleges and school sixth forms

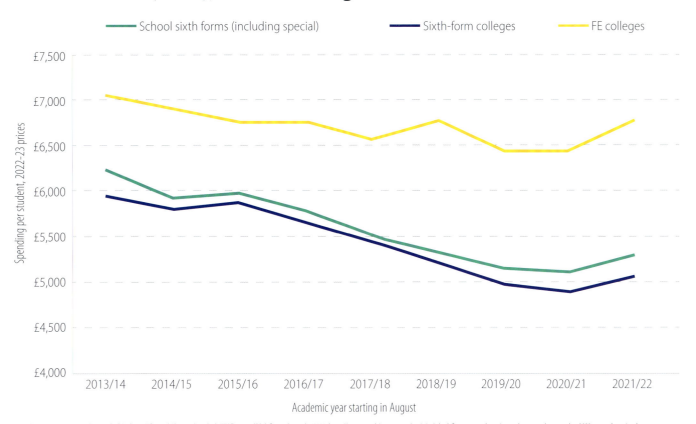

Note and source: See '16-18 spending: methods' in https://ifs.org.uk/data-and-methods; HM Treasury GDP deflators, September 2022, https://www.gov.uk/government/statistics/gdp-deflators-at-market-prices-and-money-gdp-september-2022-quarterly-national-accounts

Figure 5. Spending per student in 16-18 colleges and school sixth forms

Note and source: See '16−18 spending: methods' in https://ifs.org.uk/data-and- methods. HM Treasury GDP deflators, September2022, https://www.gov.uk/government/statistics/gdp-deflators-at-market-prices-and- money-gdp-september-2022-quarterly-national-accounts.

Forecast GDP deflators are from Citi and are those underpinning the analysis in Chapters 3 and 4 of the IFS Green Budget October 2022; they are available upon request.

spending per student was higher in colleges than in school sixth forms in 2010–11, reversing the picture over much of the 2000s when spending per student was higher in school sixth forms. This was partly a deliberate policy choice to reduce the then gap in spending between colleges and school sixth forms.

Since 2010–11, there has been a decline in per-student spending across all types of institutions. Between 2010–11 and 2019–20, spending per student fell by 14% in colleges and 28% in school sixth forms. For colleges, this left spending per student at around the level it was in 2004–05, while spending per student in sixth forms was lower than at any point since at least 2002.

As mentioned above, the government has allocated a total of £2.3 billion in additional funding for 16–18 education in 2024–25 compared with 2019–20. While this represents a significant injection of additional funding over the next few years, the effect on per-student spending is dampened by rising student numbers and rising levels of inflation.

As a result of rising student numbers and cost pressures, funding per student aged 16–18 is set to plateau after 2021–22 at just over £6,500 in colleges and around £5,200 for school sixth forms. This means that spending per pupil will remain around the same level it was in 2018–19, which is well below the high point seen in the early 2010s. As a result, spending per student aged 16–18 in colleges in 2024–25 will remain about 11% lower in real terms than it was in 2010–11, and about 27% lower in school sixth forms.

Rising costs and resource challenges

These projections up to 2024–25 are based on forecasts for economy-wide inflation (as captured by the GDP deflator) of 6% for 2022–23, just under 5% for 2023–24 and 3% for 2024–25. The key question for determining the scale of resource challenges facing colleges and sixth forms is the extent to which they actually face these levels of inflation.

For school sixth forms, there are good reasons to believe that these figures represent a fair measure of the likely inflation schools will face in the coming years. In a recent report, we estimated that schools' costs are likely to grow by 6% in 2022–23, reflecting a 5–6% increase in average teacher pay, likely increases in support staff pay of over 8%, and rising energy and food prices. We estimated that school costs are then likely to increase by a further 4% in 2023–24 and 3% in 2024–25.

The picture for colleges could be different as they are not covered by the large increases in teacher pay or support staff pay under the local government settlement. Indeed, the Association of Colleges has so far offered a headline salary rise of 2.5% for college staff in 2022–23, plus non-consolidated cost-of-living payments of £500–£750 for lower-paid staff. This has been rejected by the relevant trade unions. If this offer were delivered, then colleges would probably face a rate of inflation well below the 6% seen across the economy, on average.

There are, however, reasons to believe that the actual pay rise for college staff will need to end up higher than 2.5%. First, a tight labour market is likely to create intense competition for staff. College staff were already paid less than their counterparts in schools. Delivering a significantly lower pay award for college staff than that in schools could risk exacerbating recruitment and retention difficulties at a time when the workforce will need to expand to meet the growing student population. Second, the high level of inflation is likely to create significant pressure and expectations from college staff.

The main challenge is that colleges probably cannot afford that much more given the growth in funding per student. Precise funding allocations for 2022–23 are not yet published. However, the 2021 Spending Review settlement implies cash-terms growth in funding per student of about 4% in 2022–23. This will need to cover extra teaching hours and higher non-staff costs.

Future prospects

The future outlook for sixth forms and colleges will largely depend on the overall outlook for public spending. In his statement on 17 October, the new Chancellor, Jeremy Hunt, signalled a need for public spending cuts in order to meet the government's medium-term fiscal goals. This could include cuts to previous departmental spending plans (which currently extend up to 2024–25), as well as cuts beyond 2024–25.

Cuts are likely to be extremely hard to deliver in colleges and sixth forms, which have already seen large cuts and where spending per student has still not returned to its 2010 levels. With higher levels of inflation and growth in student numbers, current plans imply a real-terms freeze in spending per student between now and 2024–25. Any reductions in spending plans would therefore imply a return to real-terms cuts in spending per student. Furthermore, a projected 2% rise in the student population between 2024 and 2026 will make it even more difficult to deliver falls in total spending after 2024.

24 October 2022

This is also co-funded by the ESRC through the IAA, grant ref ES/T50192X/1

Key Facts

- Since the mid 1980s, the proportion of 16- and 17-year-olds in full-time education has more than doubled from around 40% to 84%.

- Between 2019 and 2022, the number of 16- and 17-year-olds in England grew by 9% or an additional 110,000 young people.

- Since 2010–11, there has been a decline in per-student spending across all types of institutions. Between 2010–11 and 2019–20, spending per student fell by 14% in colleges and 28% in school sixth forms.

www.ifs.org.uk

The new enlightened education: diversity over competition

By Shannon Rawlins

Currently, the foundation of the UK education system, across all levels, is competition. Students are ranked against one another and compete for grades. In the end, it all boils down to the day when you receive that sheet of paper which tells you whether all the slogging was worth it. Inevitably, some will be elated and others will be disappointed; not everyone can achieve the top grades. The objective of giving education is reduced to churning out numbers to move students on to the next stage. Everything comes down to assessments, meaning all forms of achievement are made quantifiable. Often, this means that what students are taught is not applicable to contexts beyond examinations. The challenge is simply to regurgitate under exam conditions.

Reform fails to perform

The reformed GCSEs and A Levels have made examinations even more tough, competitive and stressful. According to the OECD, since 2015 (the year the reforms came into effect), the life satisfaction of the UK's 15-year-olds has declined the most out of any country. The reforms have made the curriculum narrower and more compartmentalised, to the point that it dissuades deep understanding and independent thinking. Moreover, 73 per cent of teachers believe student mental health has worsened among students since the introduction of the reformed GCSEs.

This focus on classification and competition reflects the reality of capitalism and the values of the European Age of Enlightenment, such as quantification, equality of opportunity and empiricism. The root problem with such a system is that it assumes there is a level playing field and ignores the reality of diversity. Some kids are naturally 'book smart,' and are easily able to recall facts and information, while others are not. Some kids benefit from a nurturing home environment and others do not. Some schools are better than others. The quality of teachers varies greatly. Some students work well under timed conditions and others do not. All of this means that the system is too arbitrary and ultimately unfair.

Useless knowledge

The argument for competition in education is that it drives excellence and prepares young people for the harsh reality of the working world. Having achieved strong GCSE and A-Level results and then going on to Cambridge University, I am an example of someone who has thrived in competitive academic environments. Yet having come out the other side, I am disillusioned with the system. I have a string of excellent results and I am full of useless knowledge. It also goes to show how the system preserves privilege; I was able to perform well academically because I was fortunate to go to a good school and blessed with supportive, encouraging parents.

In 1980, only 15 per cent of students went on to study at university; now, over half go on to higher education.

Moreover, 60 per cent of those from independent schools attend a Russell Group university, and just under a quarter of those come from comprehensives and sixth-form colleges.

As more and more students excel academically, the justification for a competition-based education system weakens. Now, achieving A grades at A-Level and getting a degree from a good university hardly sets you apart from others.

Ticking all the right boxes

The obsession with numerical assessment, which characterises the UK education system, also stifles independent thinking – particularly for arts and humanities subjects. Students end up learning fixed formulaic methods for answering essay questions because they see it as the only way to achieve high marks. This means they can never really tap into the meaningful depths of literature and history because they are so preoccupied with the need to produce an answer under timed conditions which ticks all the right boxes.

Advocates of examination-based learning would argue that there is no other way to incentivise and challenge students to do better and work harder. However, this tends to have a negative impact on student wellbeing. Around 15 per cent of GCSE students fall under the category of being 'highly test anxious.' Two-thirds of children rank homework and exams as their greatest cause of stress.

The argument for tough, memory-based exams is also based on an assumption that the goal of education is for students to perform well in assessments. But what if the purpose of education was reformulated? What if the objective of education was to produce secure, empathetic, resilient and self-aware individuals? What if education actually supported students' mental health, rather than making it worse?

I feel that an education which taught me how to relate to others and how to be mindful would have better prepared me for the world. We have come a long way since the Age of Enlightenment, and it is high time for a new set of values.

This means moving away from the endless emphasis on quantifiable testing, and towards a system with more opportunities for creativity and practical work. This also means celebrating diversity and enabling students to specialise and learn in an individualised way which suits their particular needs and skillset. Finally, it means allowing all pupils to flourish, rather than punitively categorising students according to how they perform in stressful, time-pressured exams.

17 June 2022

www.shoutoutuk.org

International baccalaureate: how the media helps the qualification retain prestige

An article from The Conversation.

By Saira Fitzgerald, Visiting Postdoctoral Research Fellow in the ESRC Centre for Corpus Approaches to Social Science, Lancaster University

More than 150 countries around the world offer school pupils the opportunity to take the international baccalaureate (IB) rather than qualifications from their own education systems.

The IB is a series of educational programmes for students aged from three to 19. It was originally created to serve a mobile international clientele, such as the children of diplomats, who needed a kind of academic passport as they moved from one country to another. In order to serve this transient population, the IB was primarily taught in private international schools around the world.

Things have changed since those early days when the IB was a niche product in elite schools. Today, IB programs serve a variety of needs in different countries. More than half of the 5,500 schools worldwide offering the qualification are state-funded.

In these cases, the IB forms part of the local education system and is funded using public money. In the UK, the most common route is to take the IB diploma as an alternative to A-levels.

High reputation

Over the last five decades, the IB has developed a reputation as a high-status qualification. Official descriptions present the IB as doing more than other education options, providing students with the best preparation for university and employment, and overall as being better than the UK's national curriculum.

As a global product, the IB takes great care to promote a consistent brand image, with emphasis on its reliability and consistent high standards. A testimonial on the IB website praises this notion of a uniform product.

But what gets lost in these descriptions is that each national situation is unique. During the pandemic, when the IB cancelled examinations, they came up with a 'bespoke equation' for every school because each school context was different.

My research has looked at five decades of media representation of the IB on a global scale as a way to explore everyday language used to talk about the IB. I used the global press as a window into public opinion. I analysed 29,491 articles, including letters to the editor, obituaries and editorials, from 916 newspapers in 55 countries. I found that national education is frequently compared negatively to the IB.

For example, a comparison between the IB and American education system described the IB as the 'educational equivalent of a power breakfast, lunch, and dinner' as opposed to the 'cafeteria style' curriculum of state education that lacked focus, rigour and academic content.

When the IB was compared to other education systems, words such as 'prestigious' and 'rigorous' typically occurred in relation to the IB. These repeated positive references to the IB make other curricula appear inferior or deficient.

I also found recurring emphasis on the 'international' aspect of the IB. This makes the IB seem more global in

scope, capable of holding students, schools and teachers to international standards. In contrast, national curriculums seem insular and narrow.

The IB's international dimension was further emphasised by frequent references to Switzerland, such as describing it as the 'Swiss-based' or 'Geneva-based' international baccalaureate. These typically occurred in descriptions relating that the IB began in Geneva. Descriptions of the IB as a non-profit organisation based in Switzerland convey the image of a United Nations-type body, a connection founded on the presence of key UN offices in Switzerland.

The emphasis on Switzerland also masks the fact that half of the IB World Schools – the schools that offer the IB – are located in North America. This is important because it helps contribute to the idea of a uniform IB brand.

I also found the repeated use of 'IB' as a label, in reference to the curriculum (IB program), institutions (IB organisation), awards (IB certificate) and people (IB student). This formulaic way of talking about different aspects of the IB repeats across countries and creates a unified 'IB World'. The positive values and attitudes that have become associated with the IB label ensure that its reputation is amplified on the global stage as everyone talks about it in the same way.

There are many reasons why students choose the IB. One reason may be that national education systems keep getting portrayed in negative terms in the media, with emphasis on falling standards or that education is in crisis. These representations are heightened in comparison to the IB.

1 November 2022

Key Fact

- More than 150 countries around the world offer school pupils the opportunity to take the Internatational Baccalaureate (IB) rather than qualifications from their own education systems.

Design

Create a leaflet that outlines the difference between A-levels and the International Baccalaureate.

THE CONVERSATION

www.theconversation.com

Easy A-levels and lazy students: do high grades even count?

By Lucy Farmer

A-Level students don't have to worry about Covid-19 anymore; the country is convinced they're plagued by another contagion. That is, a fresh bout of laziness forcing the government to dial down exam pressure and make Sixth Form a breeze.

But amidst this mad political squabble over children's qualifications, people seem to have forgotten the tough and determined experiences of the very students they intend to belittle.

Unattainable exam excellence

According to a survey conducted by the *Sunday Times*, 41 per cent of participants believed A-Levels have gotten easier, compared to a measly 9 per cent concluding they've gotten harder.

Participants aged 18-24, however, were far more likely to say exams have gotten harder, totalling at 19 per cent. This is no coincidental divide. An analysis of this could go on and on. Wash away all the false claims and clown make-up of these governmental figures, and you realise people writing these laws will never have to go through the horror of taking these reformed A-Levels.

They will never sit on a small, wobbling table in a damp gymnasium and have their hands shake as they scribble out answers on a paper designed to trip them up. Nor will they face the barrage of complaints and spiteful comments against them when their results come out higher than ever before.

So why should they be the ones to dictate how hard A-Level examinations should become? A culture of mobile phones and instant entertainment has not suddenly polluted young people into becoming idle. Most students don't sit in puddles of their own drool and prop their feet up on stacks of unopened textbooks, impatiently awaiting their A*s. Good grades are harder to maintain than getting a flock of disgruntled politicians to agree on something. In fact, since 2008, the distribution of grades achieved has been almost static – consistently holding students in scarily high expectations.

A deterioration of merit

The one leg that this idea of easy A-Levels has to stand on is a study conducted by Loughborough University, concluding that the standards of taking A-Levels have been in gradual decline since the 1960s. It's most definitely true that a higher percentage of graduates are achieving the infamous, controversial A and A* grades. But this does not immediately point huge, neon signs at the inherent laziness of upcoming students.

For one, this decline only took place between the 1960s and 1990s, leaving a 30-year gap in which no decrease in standards took place. That's enough years for someone to graduate, claw their way up the political career path and sit idly while complaining that better grades and higher university admissions is the fault of a rowdy and ungrateful generation.

Considering the worrying estimate of 3,000 students a year calling Childline with extreme cases of exam anxiety and stress, it's easy to conclude that the pressures and expectations placed on aspiring A-Level students have not decreased despite this myth of easy exams.

But, it's simpler to disregard the mental wellbeing of an entire generation in favour of an abundance of statistics.

The growth of expectations

Grade inflation is an undeniable phenomenon. With the 1987 grade allocation quotas being abolished, the sharp increase in students being awarded Bs and above was evident. Take the 17.7 per cent increase in achievement of A or A* grades between 1982 and 2012.

Now with a grade system neither completely norm-referenced or criterion-referenced, it's become commonplace to assume governments are inflating the number of higher grades achieved to counteract dumber and dumber students lumbering their way into Sixth Form. All in the name of international recognition and a Gold Star for their DIY unemployment solution.

But this washed-out manner of observing the statistics does not address the growth of university applications, and how this is tightening grade standards like an uncomfortable noose around the neck of students. There has been a net increase of approximately 301,000 university applications between 1994 and 2019. That's 301,000 excuses for universities to be pickier, and fall into the trap of creating excessive pressure on young people.

Celebrating success

The increasing availability of knowledge and resources has opened the opportunity of higher education to minorities and lower-income households otherwise historically refused access to qualifications, paving the way for an economy of equality. But the cycle is vicious. Though more students can apply, top universities become stricter in their admissions, and suddenly the expectation is to score higher and higher.

More and more students can now march their way through A-Levels with confident stride. Pick up a sparkler and rejoice in that fact. Don't use it as another way to berate the young for a system they do not control.

Education is one of the only things in the economy that trickles down successfully. You can see with the economic rise of South Korea and Japan – countries somewhat devoid of those tasty natural resources to fatten up their wallet – and how this boils down to a realisation that, 'oh dear, maybe we should be helping our citizens develop mentally instead of stepping on them for outdoing us?'

As a country, our goal should be exactly that. We must reduce suffering and make things a little easier for the next in-line, even if that means admitting the upcoming generations might just outshine us.

20 October 2020

www.shoutoutuk.org

Former education ministers attack plan to reduce vocational qualifications

Coalition fears DfE may break pledges that only small percentage of qualifications will be replaced by T-levels.

By Richard Adams, Education Editor

A coalition of former education ministers has attacked the government's 'disastrous' plan to scrap dozens of popular vocational qualifications in England and push students into taking its favoured new T-levels.

David Blunkett, the former Labour education secretary, said he feared that widespread scrapping of qualifications such as BTecs from 2025 could backfire and lead to more 17 and 18-year-olds opting to take A-levels rather than the vital vocational qualifications the country needs.

'At this moment in time, every high quality route to employment and filling the vast vacancies which exist should be encouraged rather than abolished, and clear commitments given in parliament should be honoured,' Lord Blunkett said.

A joint letter from the group to the education secretary, Gillian Keegan, accuses the Department for Education (DfE) of breaking earlier pledges that only a small percentage of the applied qualifications would have their funding cut off and replaced by T-levels.

The signatories alongside Blunkett and Ken Baker, who served as education secretary under Margaret Thatcher, include David Willetts and Jo Johnson, the former Conservative education ministers, and Sue Garden, the

Liberal Democrat peer and deputy speaker of the House of Lords.

A copy of the letter, seen by the *Guardian*, states: 'These qualifications are popular with students, respected by employers and valued by universities. Removing them will have a disastrous impact on social mobility, economic growth and our public services.

'For example, it is difficult to think of a worse time to scrap the extended diploma in health and social care. Given their importance to the healthcare workforce, it would be very damaging to the NHS to remove funding for these qualifications.'

BTecs are the most well-known applied general qualifications, with about 200,000 students each year taking BTec qualifications at level three, the equivalent to A-levels. The qualifications are nationally accepted for entry to apprenticeships and technical training, and for entry to university.

The government wants more students in England to take its T-level qualification, introduced in 2020 but so far only available in seven vocational areas, including education and childcare, construction and health and science. More subjects will be added later this year but colleges remain

Brainstorm

In small groups, discuss what you know about T-levels. What are the differences between T-levels and BTecs?

reluctant to teach them, because of lack of demand and extra expense as well as the substantial work placements they require.

Critics also say T-levels are too narrowly focused, with each T-level the equivalent of three A-level or BTec subjects, meaning students can take only a single course after they finish GCSEs.

The government had promised that the funding of BTecs and similar qualifications would be protected while T-levels were being rolled out. In April last year, both Nadhim Zahawi, the then education secretary, and Diana Barran, the education minister in the Lords, said during debates in parliament that only 'a small proportion of applied general qualifications would be removed'.

But in January, a DfE guide included a list of subjects where ministers had made a 'conscious choice' to axe funding, which researchers found would mean cutting 75 out of 134 relevant qualifications.

The letter urges Keegan to exempt all 134 qualifications from the cull, saying that they remain 'a vital pathway to higher education and employment' for many young people.

Blunkett said: 'A failure to listen to what business is saying and ensure there is real choice – which of course would include T-levels – is damaging to the economy, and a complete contradiction to the thrust of Jeremy Hunt's speech last Friday.'

The Labour peer warned that reducing student choice to A-levels or T-levels could backfire. 'I fear that government has still not understood that the route to T-levels is now

being toughened to the point where applying for A-levels is actually easier,' he said.

Bill Watkin, the chief executive of the Sixth Form Colleges Association – which is leading a campaign to protect student choice by retaining BTecs – said scrapping so many valued qualifications in the space of two years was 'utterly unacceptable'.

'Unless the government reverses this decision, and starts to incorporate some evidence and transparency into its policymaking, tens of thousands of students will be left without a pathway to higher education or employment, and many employers will be left without the skilled workforce they need,' he said.

A DfE spokesperson said: 'Our reforms will simplify the system for young people, with popular BTecs continuing to be available alongside A-levels and T levels. The BTecs that will no longer be available are only those with low take-up, poor outcomes, or which overlap with T-levels. We have also introduced a transition year to support students who may have taken BTecs, into T-level qualifications.

'We are committed to creating a world-class education system that provides a ladder up for all and gives young people the skills and knowledge to prepare them for higher education and the world of work.'

29 January 2023

'Arts subjects have as much value as STEM': the new education campaign tackling the myth of 'soft' degrees

A new initiative aiming to put humanities and arts subjects on a par with STEM disciplines is long overdue, according to these experts.

By Katie Russell

It's the question every English Literature graduate is familiar with. 'Oh, so do you want to be a teacher?'

It was a question I grew tired of hearing at every house party or family gathering while studying English Literature at the University of Exeter.

It's not that I felt insulted. It's just that I know for a fact I don't have the patience or thick skin to be a teacher – so it was frustrating for people to imply that was all I was qualified to do.

Still, that was better than the comments from Medicine and Engineering students, who would make quips like, 'All you do is read novels and write down your opinion? Anyone could do that.'

Students and graduates of arts, humanities and social science degrees are used to being made to feel like they chose life's soft option. So a new campaign to give those subjects the recognition and kudos they deserve is very welcome indeed, and long overdue.

The campaign SHAPE (standing for Social Sciences, Humanities and the Arts for People and the Economy) is spearheaded by the London School of Economics, alongside the Academy of Social Sciences, the British Academy and Arts Council England.

Uniting these disciplines under one acronym (just as the STEM campaign united science, technology, engineering and maths), they have created a 'shorthand way of describing them, which can unite them and celebrate their value', explains Julia Black, professor of law at LSE and fellow of the British Academy.

'It gives them a coherence,' Black explains, 'in the same way that STEM has given a hugely heterogeneous group of subjects a coherence around what it is that they're exploring – even though they themselves are hugely varied.'

The link between all SHAPE subjects, she adds, is that they 'focus on people and societies'.

However, Black insists that SHAPE has not been launched to directly rival STEM. 'We're not saying that SHAPE subjects are better than STEM,' she says, but the campaign is an attempt to 'level up' SHAPE subjects, and prove they 'have as much value' as STEM subjects.

So, just as governments and academic institutions ran campaigns and initiatives to encourage more young people to pursue STEM subjects over the past two decades, does the launch of SHAPE mean there will be a swing towards taking humanities, social sciences and arts subjects more seriously?

We talked to the experts to tackle some of the myths surrounding SHAPE subjects, to find out whether arts and humanities subjects deserve their 'soft' status, and to see how they feel about a potential reappraisal and revival.

Myth 1: Work in SHAPE subjects less skilled than in STEM

Humanities, social sciences and the arts have long been seen as 'softer' subjects, according to Black. It's an unflattering description – and one that Martyn Powell, head of Humanities at Bristol University, rallies against.

'I wouldn't describe any of the humanities subjects that I represent in my school as soft,' he says, adding that most of his humanities subjects have been part of higher education for a long time, and 'that pedigree serves subjects like history, English, philosophy exceptionally well'.

Nonetheless, these subjects are often undermined due to their interpretative and subjective nature. Yet 'people underplay the skills that are involved in the humanities', Black says.

She adds that the skills across SHAPE and STEM overlap, and 'the highest quality work and research that's being produced in humanities, social sciences or arts subjects is just as skilled as that which is being produced in STEM subjects'.

So why are humanities, and the industries humanities graduates often go into after graduating, often seen as being less important and having less value?

'Often they can get overlooked because what you're not producing is a shiny new thing,' Black explains. Humanities graduates don't tend to invent new technology, machines or medicine, for instance. Instead, 'what you're producing are changes in behaviours, social structures, the way that we govern ourselves'. Instead of inventing a new medicine, therefore, a humanities student might organise the way we manage our healthcare system.

People also overlook that the 'softer' subjects bring a huge value to the economy. Before Covid-19, for instance, the creative industries sector (in which high numbers of SHAPE graduates work) was growing at five times the rate of the rest of the economy, contributing almost £13 million to the UK economy every hour – or, £110 billion per year. This was more than automation, aerospace and life sciences combined. Most of us aren't aware of this huge contribution, however, because the 'nature of the industry is that it's a lot of very small companies', Black explains.

Myth 2: SHAPE subjects don't teach you skills for the real world

If you specialise in natural geography at university, you'll leave with more than a thorough knowledge of rock formations. Humanities are valuable because of the 'mindsets that come from studying those subjects', Black explains. Analysis, interpretation and fact-checking are useful for 'multiple walks of life,' she adds, 'including when reading news on Facebook'.

This is particularly prevalent in studying history, says Tony Grogan, a history teacher at Turton School in Greater Manchester, and an ambassador for Get Into Teaching.

'We're giving students the skills for the future, to question what's happening around them,' he says. 'We're not telling them what to think – we're giving them the tools to think it themselves.'

A subject like history allows students to be 'informed', he says – and to look at situations from other perspectives, and engage in debate. 'It's not like maths where it's black and white, right or wrong. There are so many nuances.'

Creativity, curiosity, empathy, and an acknowledgement of consequences to our actions are also skills that you can master through studying humanities, social sciences and the arts.

These skills can help you to be more outward-thinking, and learning a language is particularly important for this, as you learn about other cultures, according to Rebecca Nobes, head of Spanish at Boswells Academy in Chelmsford. 'Learning about these customs and traditions equips students with the ability to understand and accept other cultures, a skill which is vital in the modern world.'

Myth 3: SHAPE and STEM are incompatible disciplines

In recent weeks, the Black Lives Matter movement has particularly highlighted the importance of understanding history and context, according to Grogan and Black. Humanities and social sciences have also been important in the dialogue around our response to Covid-19.

'The SHAPE subjects are ultimately about people,' says Nicholas Serota, Chair of Arts Council England. 'They help us better understand ourselves and the world around us, nurture creativity, foster innovation and influence change. The unprecedented situation we are currently experiencing has shown how crucial this is – with behavioural scientists and economists advising Government on their response to Covid-19.'

Powell agrees. 'I think when it comes to picking up the pieces, examining why we were hit in the way we have been, what we're going to do next, humanities specialists will have a major part to play – historians in particular.'

The arts have had a part to play too, with people in lockdown 'consuming more creative content than ever before', Serota says. Reading books and watching shows on Netflix have given us a sense of joy in these dark times – highlighting the importance of the creative sector and, by association, the SHAPE subjects that shape it.

However, SHAPE subjects have the biggest potential for creating change when they are used in conjunction with STEM. This is why we need to 'fund work on a cross-disciplinary basis', according to Black. 'Rather than just focusing on the STEM side, if we bring in the SHAPE subjects as well then we can really start to tackle the problems that we have,' she says.

She gives the example of the current research on how Covid-19 is disproportionately affecting people from BAME backgrounds – and how social factors are at play. 'What starts out as a health question morphs into a question about socioeconomic deprivation, education, life chances, and so on.

'Which is where you then turn to SHAPE subjects to really understand what those conditions are and what some of the solutions might be.'

Myth 4: SHAPE graduates end up in low-paying jobs

This is all very well, but can you get a good job with a humanities or social sciences degree?

Last year, research from the Institute of Fiscal Studies found that those who studied English or the arts at university were likely to earn, on average, less than someone who never went to university at all. For the average man, for instance, a creative arts degree led to earning less than £25,900 a year

by the age of 29, whereas men who didn't attend university earned an average of £30,000 a year (assuming they had 5 GCSEs of A*-C grade).

This isn't the case across the board, however; as Black notes, there are high-paying jobs across STEM and SHAPE subjects – Medicine and Law, for instance, have similar earnings, and, in general, 'you don't get the level of disparity that you might think'.

'It's not necessarily the case that you do STEM, you're going to get a nice, stable, high-paying job, and you do SHAPE subjects and you're not,' Black adds. 'That's just empirically not the case.'

Humanities alumni from Bristol University have gone on to jobs in law, accounting, academia, politics and government, policy and more, according to Powell. 'A major advantage of a humanities degree that it doesn't pigeon-hole you at a very early stage into a kind of career,' he says.

History and PPE graduates are 'very prominent in the House of Commons', Powell adds, and he believes these subjects teach students the skills they need to be a leader – including 'historical skills of research analysis and rhetoric' as well as 'leadership and management', which is part of many courses.

SHAPE graduates also tend to go into the information and communications sector, according to Black, which is a 'big employer of English graduates' in particular and is a 'big sector of our economy and digital economy increasingly going forward'.

Humanities students have a place in this digital economy, according to Powell, and he says many go into the tech industry. 'It isn't just about coding,' he says.

'Social media is as much about relationship building as anything else, so anybody who's been involved in studying English Literature or History will have had a very intense experience in terms of studying relationships.

'Equally, anybody involved in the study of History, Religious Studies, English, or Classics, will have a very intense sense of narrative and the importance of framing narrative – and that's important in terms of people's profiles on social media but also in terms of the gaming industry, and a whole world of other tech-related arts.'

In other words, a humanities degree can hold the key to a number of professions – not just teaching.

25 June 2020

Consider

Do you think arts, humanities and social science degrees are as valuable as ones in STEM subjects? In pairs, discuss this topic and feedback your thoughts to the rest of the class.

No staring out of the window! Why super-strict schools are on the rise

Blind rule-following may improve grades but does it stamp out individuality? A teacher who has seen the results discusses the pros and cons.

By Lucy Kellaway

In my first term as a trainee teacher, I was standing at the front of the classroom trying to prove to a year 7 class that 0.1 is bigger than 0.0999. Unannounced, in walked a deputy principal who stood at the back, glowering.

After a few minutes she stopped the lesson. 'Miss!' she hissed. 'Didn't you see what just happened there? This young man [pointing at a luckless child in the front row] drank some water from his bottle!' She removed the offending boy from the class and told me she would speak to me later.

This took place at one of the most famously strict schools in the country. The rules at this school are innumerable and mostly about very small things, including the stipulation that no child can have a sip of water in a lesson without permission.

As a strip was torn off the boy, he looked as if he was going to cry. Had I been a younger trainee, rather than a 58-year-old, I might have cried, too, but as it was I felt furious.

What a stupid rule, I fumed. All that matters is that this boy understands decimals. If he wants some water, where's the harm?

I thought about this incident last week when I read about a school in Leicestershire, John Ferneley College, where children are said to be forced to smile and are banned from looking out of the window. According to reports, students must maintain eye contact with their teacher when they are

talking, and if a member of staff says hello to students they should make sure their reply is 'upbeat'. On a community Facebook page, some parents have said the rules make the school seem 'like some sort of prison camp'.

This is the latest in many such stories that pop up each time another school goes super-strict – and the outrage is always the same. We are teaching children to be robots! We don't treat our pets like this!

When I had my first brush with strictness, I saw it like that, too. But having spent the past four years teaching under this unforgiving regime, I have largely changed my mind.

The first thing in their favour is that these rules work – if by 'work' you mean that they lead to great exam results. The school I trained in used to be one of the most unruly in the country; when it was shut down in 1995 students were three years behind the average national reading age. It reopened in 2004 with the same sort of students, but a new set of rules outlawing talking in corridors and looking out of windows – with the result that the school is at the top of the national exam league tables. This is a triumph for social mobility – a large number of students, many of whom are on free school meals, go on to Russell group universities. Every year a handful get into Oxbridge.

It's no secret that strictness and results are linked – and as schools are now judged entirely on exam results, more are copying the super-strict model. But in this scramble for

Three schools and their very strict rules

Michaela Community School, Wembley, north London

Described as Britain's strictest school, the establishment is renowned for its 'silent corridor' rule. Pupils must walk between their classrooms in single file without talking, or they risk a detention. Other offences include forgetting a pen or ruler, arriving one minute late to school and even turning around in class when told not to.

King James's School, Huddersfield

In 2017, the school introduced 40 new rules under the categories of 'Manners, Uniform and Behaviour'. Some of the strictest include no slouching, no staring out of the window during lessons, no replying to questions with colloquialisms such as 'dunno' and no rolling of eyes.

Merchant's Academy, Bristol

A new set of rules in 2017 infuriated parents after pupils were removed from classrooms for clock-watching, tapping tables and having shoes that were too shiny. If their appearance wasn't up to scratch, students were made to wear lanyards that read: 'I have 24 hours to sort out my uniform.'

better grades, is there any such thing as too strict? It seems there isn't. I've visited schools that have only half adopted the rules – they have line-ups and uniform checks, but still allow students to talk in corridors – and their results aren't as good as those of the more extreme schools.

But does all this blind rule-following turn children into exam-passing robots? Not in my experience, though I sometimes regret how muted they are in class. The other day I watched through the staff room window a child who is particularly silent in my lessons making all his friends scream with laughter in the playground.

'I wish he could be himself like that in my lesson,' I said. 'Are you sure?' asked a Spanish teacher who'd spent the previous 11 years at a freewheeling school nearby. He told me that 'being themselves' meant his students would tell him to his face they couldn't be arsed to do their homework as there was no point to learning Spanish.

My second sadness is that behaviour is excellent in my school because the children are given no choice in the matter. 'Good morning Miss,' they say – not because they want to, but because they will get a detention if they don't.

This was rammed home to me two years ago when I was invited to evensong at Eton. There I saw boys in tailcoats talking (talking!) to each other as they entered the chapel, falling silent as the service began. There were no teachers shouting at them – instead I was thunderstruck to see masters chatting with their charges.

Yet these are boys who have won the birth lottery. Good behaviour has always been expected of them, so when they arrive at the poshest school in the land they are treated like adults by their teachers. By contrast, many of the students at my school were born into deprivation and their reward

is to be treated like detainees. I get it, but this educational apartheid makes me very uncomfortable.

Katharine Birbalsingh, principal of Michaela Community School in Wembley, which has been described as the strictest in Britain, has often noted that in her academically brilliant school there is not one middle class white child. The parents look at this educational boot camp and think: no thanks. My hunch is that this is changing. At least at my school there are some children of QCs and university professors who have thought it through: they would rather 'strict plus good grades' than 'liberty plus rubbish ones'. Indeed, I now fancy that both my adult sons – who were lazy, indifferent students at the private schools they went to – might have done better at boot camp.

My biggest reservation is that the strict school model is too rigid and allows no space for discussion or debate. For both students and staff, fear plays a large part in upholding this culture. And while history tells us that fear can be a very powerful motivator, it doesn't inspire individuals to do their best.

The final thing that bothers me is the extremity of the reactions that super-strict schools provoke. People either believe in them completely or think they are the very devil, squashing and damaging students in pursuit of results. This is no way to arrange a debate on education. Surely different sorts of schools are good for different sorts of students – and teachers. I have learnt a lot from my strict school and am a much better teacher because of it, but it goes too much against my hippy grain – and so I'm changing schools in September.

I'm sure that the slightly freer school I'm joining will have something to learn from the strict one – and vice versa. I hardly dare suggest such a thing for fear of the rancour of my former task master, but I think it's possible to relax the rules on water bottles without bringing the whole regime crashing down.

8 July 2021

Write

Do you think your school or college is too strict or not strict enough? In small groups compile a list of the rules you are aware of at your educational setting – what would you add or take away from that list? Write up a new list of rules you would like to implement and share with the rest of the class.

The above information is reprinted with kind permission from *The Telegraph*.
© Telegraph Media Group Limited YEAR OF PUBLICATION

www.telegraph.co.uk

The UK education system preserves inequality – new report

An article from The Conversation

By Imran Tahir, Research Economist,

Institute for Fiscal Studies

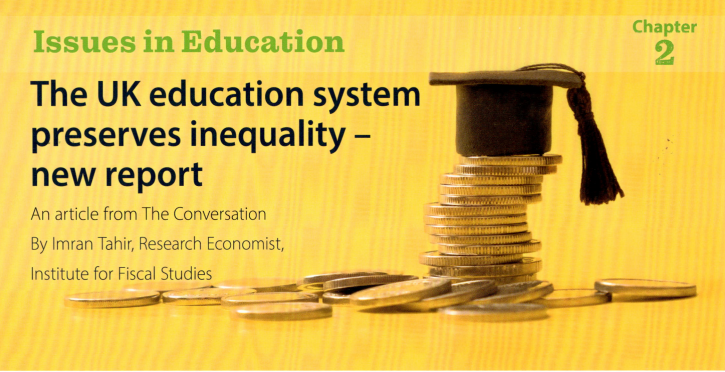

Your education has a huge effect on your life chances. As well as being likely to lead to better wages, higher levels of education are linked with better health, wealth and even happiness. It should be a way for children from deprived backgrounds to escape poverty.

However, our new comprehensive study, published as part of the Institute for Fiscal Studies Deaton Review of Inequalities, shows that education in the UK is not tackling inequality. Instead, children from poorer backgrounds do worse throughout the education system.

The report assesses existing evidence using a range of different datasets. These include national statistics published by the Department for Education on all English pupils, as well as a detailed longitudinal sample of young people from across the UK. It shows there are pervasive and entrenched inequalities in educational attainment.

Unequal success

Children from disadvantaged households tend to do worse at school. This may not be a surprising fact, but our study illustrates the magnitude of this disadvantage gap. The graph below shows that children who are eligible for free school meals (which corresponds to roughly the 15% poorest pupils) in England do significantly worse at every stage of school.

Even at the age of five, there are significant differences in achievement at school. Only 57% of children who are eligible

Attainment gaps between students eligible and not eligible for free school meals at different stages of the education system 2019

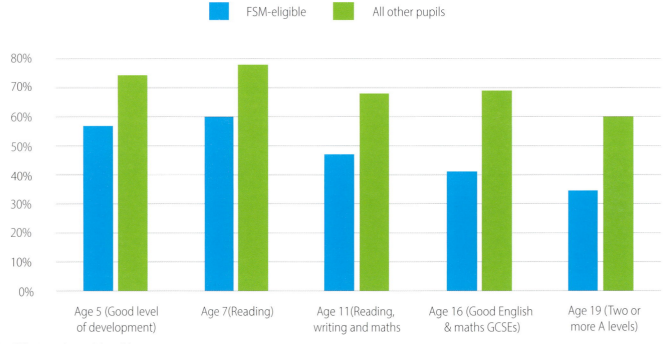

Source: IFS Education inequalities report, Author provided.

GCSE performance by children's eligibility for free school meals

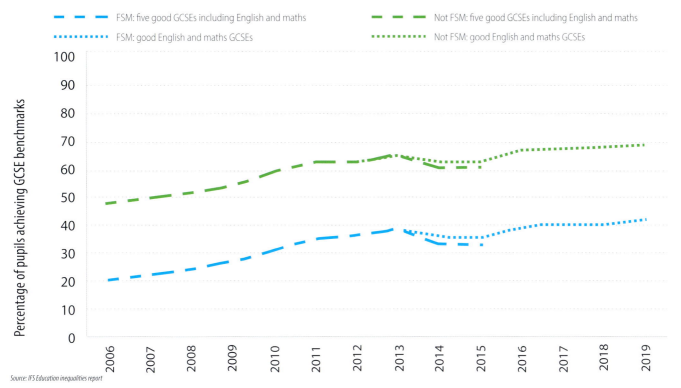

Source: IFS Education inequalities report

for free school meals are assessed as having a good level of development in meeting early learning goals, compared with 74% of children from better off households. These inequalities persist through primary school, into secondary school and beyond.

Differences in educational attainment aren't a new phenomenon. What's striking, though, is how the size of the disadvantage gap has remained constant over a long period of time. The graph above shows the percentage of students in England reaching key GCSE benchmarks by their eligibility for free school meals from the mid-2000s.

Over the past 15 years, the size of the gap in GCSE attainment between children from rich and poor households has barely

changed. Although the total share of pupils achieving these GCSE benchmarks has increased over time, children from better-off families have been 27%-28% more likely to meet these benchmarks throughout the period.

Household income

While eligibility for free school meals is one way of analysing socio-economic inequalities, it doesn't capture the full distribution of household income. Another way is to group young people according to their family income. The graph below shows young people grouped by decile. This means that young people are ordered based on their family's income at age 14 and placed into ten equal groups.

GCSE attainment by decile of household income at age 14

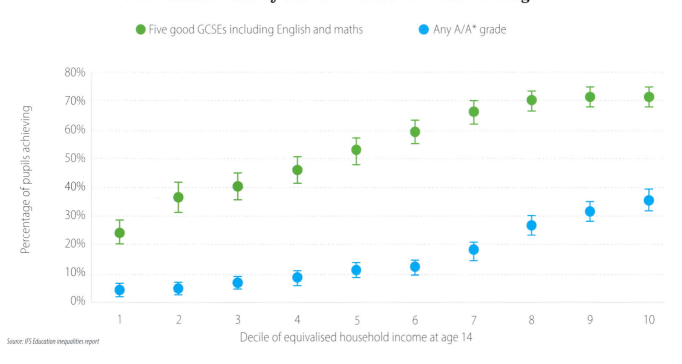

Source: IFS Education inequalities report

Distribution of highest educational attainment among 26-year-olds in England by socio-economic status, 2016.

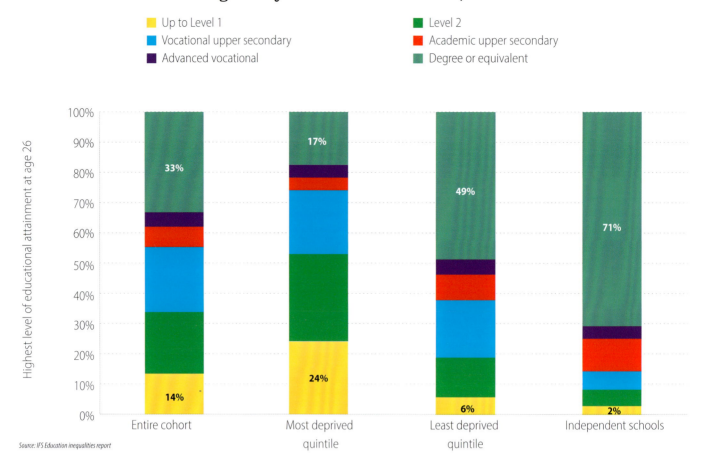

Legend:
- Up to Level 1 (yellow)
- Vocational upper secondary (blue)
- Advanced vocational (dark purple)
- Level 2 (green)
- Academic upper secondary (red)
- Degree or equivalent (teal)

Y-axis: Highest level of educational attainment at age 26 (0% to 100%)

X-axis categories: Entire cohort, Most deprived quintile, Least deprived quintile, Independent schools

Entire cohort: 14%, 33%
Most deprived quintile: 24%, 17%
Least deprived quintile: 6%, 49%
Independent schools: 2%, 71%

Source: IFS Education inequalities report

The graph shows the percentage of young people in the UK obtaining five good GCSEs, and the share obtaining at least one A or A* grade at GCSE, by the decile of their family income. With every increase in their family's wealth, children are more likely to do better at school.

More than 70% of children from the richest tenth of families earn five good GCSEs, compared with fewer than 30% in the poorest households. While just over 10% of young people in middle-earning families (and fewer than 5% of those in the poorest families) earned at least one A or A* grade at GCSE, over a third of pupils from the richest tenth of families received at least one top grade.

Inequalities into adulthood

The gaps between poor and rich children during the school years translate into huge differences in their qualifications as adults. The graph above shows educational attainment ten years after GCSEs (at the age of 26) for a group of students who took their GCSE exams in 2006.

The four bars show the distribution of qualifications at age 26 separately for the entire group, people who grew up in the poorest fifth of households, those who grew up in the richest fifth of households, and those who attended private schools.

There is a strong relationship between family background and eventual educational attainment. More than half of children who grew up in the most deprived households hold qualifications of up to GCSE level or below. On the other hand, almost half of those from the richest households have graduated from university.

The gap between private school students and the most disadvantaged is even more stark. Over 70% of private school students are university graduates by the age of 26, compared with less than 20% of children from the poorest fifth of households.

Young people from better-off families do better at all levels of the education system. They start out ahead and they end up being more qualified as adults. Instead of being an engine for social mobility, the UK's education system allows inequalities at home to turn into differences in school achievement. This means that all too often, today's education inequalities become tomorrow's income inequalities.

18 August 2022

Key Facts

- Children from disadvantaged households tend to do worse at school.

- More than 70% of children from the richest tenth of families earn five good GCSEs, compared with fewer than 30% in the poorest households.

- Young people from better-off families do better at all levels of the education system. They start out ahead and they end up being more qualified as adults.

THE CONVERSATION

www.theconversation.com

Student wellbeing at secondary school: 79% of 14 year olds extremely dissatisfied

Student wellbeing drops sharply after starting secondary school with most adolescents satisfied at 11 and most extremely dissatisfied by 14.

According to new research published in the British Journal of Developmental Psychology, student wellbeing experiences a sharp decline when students begin secondary school, regardless of background or experiences.

Academics from the Universities of Manchester and Cambridge analysed student wellbeing and self-esteem of more than 11,000 young people from across the UK, using data collected when they were 11 and again when they were 14.

It may sound shocking that at 11, most adolescents were satisfied with life, but only three years later, at 14, the majority were extremely dissatisfied by age 14. By that age, the 'subjective wellbeing' scores of 79% of participants fell below what had been the average score for the entire group three years earlier.

The study also recorded information regarding adolescents' satisfaction with specific aspects of their lives, such as:

- Schoolwork
- Personal appearance
- Family and friends

The most dramatic downturns between 11 and 14 were probably related to school and peer relationships.

Family life and economics influence student wellbeing

Circumstances such as family life and economics are widely accepted to influence young people's mental health. The

research shows that notwithstanding this, wellbeing tends to fall steeply and across the board during early adolescence.

Scientists believe the decline is probably linked to the transition to secondary school at age 11. The study identified that the aspects of wellbeing which changed in early adolescence were typically related to school and peer relationships, suggesting a close connection with shifts in these young people's academic and social lives.

In addition, students with higher self-esteem at age 11 experienced a less significant drop in wellbeing at age 14, which indicates that structured efforts to strengthen adolescents' self-esteem – particularly during the first years of secondary school – could mitigate the likely downturn in wellbeing and life satisfaction.

How can schools support student wellbeing?

The researchers have identified various ways in which schools can support student wellbeing, including:

- Celebrating students' achievements
- Reinforcing the value of things they had done well
- Avoiding comparing to other students

Adolescents' wellbeing is in decline. The Children's Society has shown that, in the UK, 12% of young people aged 10 to 17 have poor wellbeing.

'We urgently need to do more to support students' wellbeing at secondary school'

'Until now, we haven't fully understood how universally poor wellbeing is experienced,' said Dr Jose Marquez from The University of Manchester. 'The relationship between wellbeing and self-esteem has also been unclear.'

'Even though this was a large, diverse group of adolescents, we saw a consistent fall in wellbeing,' said Ioannis Katsantonis from the University of Cambridge.

'One of the most striking aspects was the clear association with changes at school. It suggests we urgently need to do more to support students' wellbeing at secondary schools across the UK.'

24 November 2022

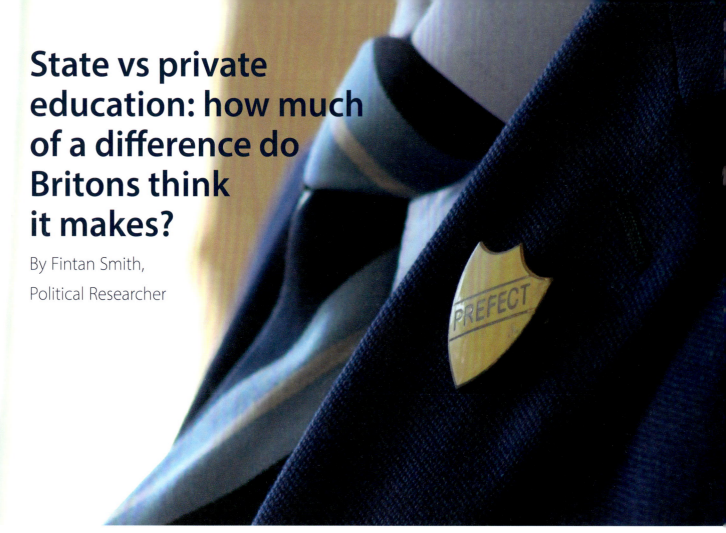

State vs private education: how much of a difference do Britons think it makes?

By Fintan Smith,
Political Researcher

With the recent release of data showing that some state schools are outperforming private schools for offers to attend Oxford or Cambridge University, The Times reported that rich parents are worried that private school may no longer be the ticket to an elite institution it once was.

That attending an expensive school might not benefit a child is nevertheless a niche view, according to new YouGov data on education quality.

Our research finds that the majority (54%) of adults in Britain believe that the quality of education they received at their secondary school was either 'very good' (20%) or 'pretty good' (34%). Three in ten (31%) think it was average, and 12% believe the education they received was bad.

However, the answer seems to heavily depend on what type of school you went to.

Of those who attended a comprehensive school, just 45% reported that the education they received was good. For those who attended a grammar school, however, this figure is much higher, at 80%. This number is similar for those who attended a private school, of whom 77% rate their education as being good.

Those who went to a comprehensive were also the most likely to rate their education as being bad (15%) compared to private school (4%) and grammar school attendees (5%).

What impact does school type have on career success?

Where the debate around the existence of grammar and private school becomes most contentious is the implication for pupil's career success. Research by the Sutton Trust has found that a disproportionate number of well-paid jobs are occupied by the privately educated, for example finding that almost three quarters (74%) of top judges were educated privately.

Our research shows a large proportion of those who were state educated believe the type of school they went to has had an impact on their career success.

Of those who attended a comprehensive, 44% believe their job prospects would have been better if they had attended a private school, 36% their career would have turned out much the same and only 3% believing they would have done worse.

They are less likely to believe going to a grammar school would have made any difference to their career than they are to believe going to a private school would have. Only a third (34%) believe they would have done better at a grammar school, with 44% believing they would have done much the same and just 3% believing they would have done worse.

When it comes to former grammar school pupils, they are much less likely than former comprehensive pupils to think their life would have been better had they attended a private school (27%). Half believe they would have done much the same (49%).

Should they have attended a comprehensive, rather than grammar school, one in three former grammar pupils believe their lives would have turned out worse as a result. Four in ten (41%) believe things would have panned out much the same.

About 80% of those who went to private or grammar schools say they got a good education — fewer than half who had a comprehensive education say the same

How good or bad an education do you think was available at the secondary school you attended?
% of 2,074 Britons who attended a non-selective state school, 646 who attended a selective state school and 253 who went to private school.

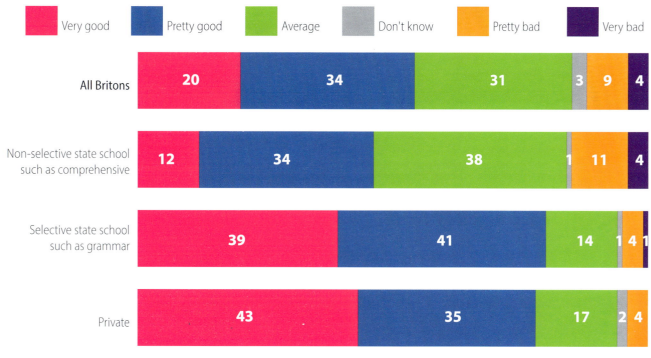

Very good | Pretty good | Average | Don't know | Pretty bad | Very bad

All Britons: 20 | 34 | 31 | 3 | 9 | 4

Non-selective state school such as comprehensive: 12 | 34 | 38 | 1 | 11 | 4

Selective state school such as grammar: 39 | 41 | 14 | 1 | 4 | 1

Private: 43 | 35 | 17 | 2 | 4

Source: YouGov: 21 Dec 2020-21 Jan 2021

Do Britons think they could have had a better career if they went to a different type of school?

Do you think you would have done better, or worse, or much the same in your career if you had gone to a... % of 2,073 Britons who attended a state non-selective school, 296 who attended private school/college, and 710 who attended a state selective school/college

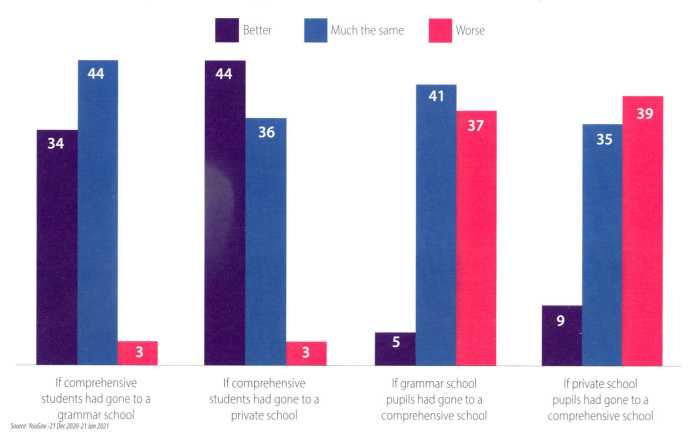

Better | Much the same | Worse

If comprehensive students had gone to a grammar school: 34 | 44 | 3

If comprehensive students had gone to a private school: 44 | 36 | 3

If grammar school pupils had gone to a comprehensive school: 5 | 41 | 37

If private school pupils had gone to a comprehensive school: 9 | 35 | 39

Source: YouGov -21 Dec 2020-21 Jan 2021

Three quarters of Britons think the kind of school a child goes to has a large/some impact on their success, but teaching standards and children's intelligence are seen as more important

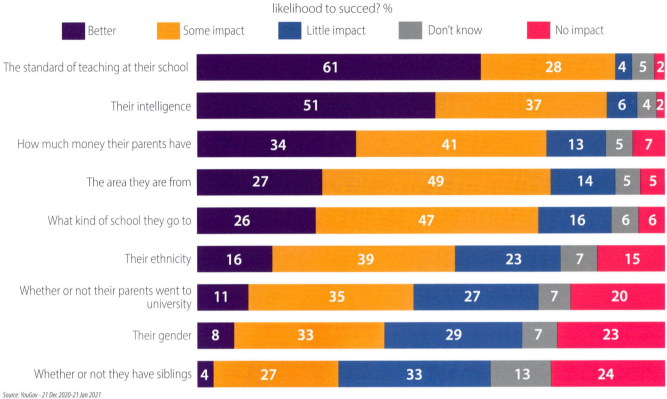

In Britain how much of an impact do you think the following factors have on children's likelihood to succeed? %

Legend: ■ Better ■ Some impact ■ Little impact ■ Don't know ■ No impact

Factor	Better	Some impact	Little impact	Don't know	No impact
The standard of teaching at their school	61	28	4	5	2
Their intelligence	51	37	6	4	2
How much money their parents have	34	41	13	5	7
The area they are from	27	49	14	5	5
What kind of school they go to	26	47	16	6	6
Their ethnicity	16	39	23	7	15
Whether or not their parents went to university	11	35	27	7	20
Their gender	8	33	29	7	23
Whether or not they have siblings	4	27	33	13	24

Source: YouGov - 21 Dec 2020-21 Jan 2021

By contrast, four in ten private school attendees (39%) think they would have done worse at a state comp, compared to 35% who think they would have done just as well.

The vast majority of Britons think the school a child attends has an impact on their success – but other factors are seen as more important still

Three quarters of Britons believe the school a child attends has a large impact (26%) or some impact (47%) on their chance of success. Only one in six (16%) think it has little impact, and just 6% say it has no impact at all.

Britons are, however, more likely to believe that the standard of teaching at school (89%) and a child's own intelligence (88%) have a large or some impact on their success.

Similar numbers of people also believe that where a child lives and grows up and the amount of money their parents have has as much of an impact on them as where they go to school, at 76% and 75% respectively.

A majority (55%) also think a child's ethnicity has a large or moderate impact, while 41% think their gender plays into children's success (with women more likely to think so than men, at 46% vs 35%).

Britons are split on the future of private and state selective schools

Despite the amount of influence Britons believe a school has on their future chances of success, there is limited support for phasing out private or state selective schools. On the question of banning private schools, just 21% would support a ban, while 30% would oppose it.

In her time as Prime Minister, Theresa May set aside money for the opening of new selective schools, paving the way for a new generation of grammar schools. Britons are divided on this issue. One in five (20%) support the status quo, saying we should keep the current number of grammar schools and not open any more. Three in ten (29%) support opening more selective schools, while a similar number (27%) believe grammar schools should be scrapped altogether.

Unsurprisingly, opinion differs between those who attended a grammar school versus those who attended a non-selective state school. Of those who attended a grammar school, 47% support the building of further such schools, while just 22% of those who attended a non-selective state school feel the same.

16 April 2021

Hannah Fry: studying maths until 18 will traumatise teenagers – not transform Britain

Rishi Sunak has pledged that all school children must continue maths after GCSE level. Mathematician Hannah Fry says it will cause more harm than good.

By Hannah Fry

I have been a professor of mathematics for a decade, and I am well aware that maths has traumatised school children for years. Ask an adult what their childhood memories are of the subject and it is never apathetic. They either loved it or they hated it. Those that hated it remember it with pain.

So I was surprised to learn about Rishi Sunak's new policy announcement, in which he has pledged that all school pupils will be made to study mathematics up to the age of 18, in a bid to combat numeracy rates. Currently in the UK, eight million adults only possess the skill level of primary school pupils.

Undoubtedly Sunak has picked up on something really important. The UK's school children are unprepared for our data-driven world. The workforce has changed, and the world has changed. Twenty years ago, you could have enjoyed a successful career without ever having to touch maths. But today that is far from the case.

There's so much data and so much quantitative analysis required in the working world, from computer science to digital strategy. Sunak is right that we should be upskilling our young people. We should be preparing them better for a data-led economy.

But is forcing school children to do a subject they hate until they are 18 years old really the silver bullet to solve all our problems? I don't think so.

The UK is currently experiencing a teaching shortage: in particular, we are struggling with a shortage of maths teachers. I have heard countless stories of PE teachers or English teachers – who have admitted that they struggle with the subject matter themselves – covering classes because there is no one else available. In fact, research by the Nuffield Foundation suggests that almost half of secondary schools are using non-specialist teachers for maths lessons.

It's probably not surprising that Sunak, much like a large chunk of our politicians, went to a top private school, Winchester College. Of course, schools such as Winchester have incredible maths teachers. The school has teachers from all walks of life who inspire them and show them how recreational maths can be.

They stretch them when they want to be stretched and support them when students want to be supported. Even better, private schools are able to offer this to every single student. Right now, that is an impossible fantasy at schools that are understaffed and struggling to simply fill a maths teacher position.

A change needs to happen. Firstly, Sunak is right that we need to improve numeracy levels. But we need to do this to make sure that our students are better prepared for the workforce we are currently in rather than the one that existed when education was designed. There are lessons currently on the maths syllabus that are really now redundant.

Some theories are largely archaic: the average person has never done a circle theorem outside of the classroom. In order to prepare students for the modern workforce we need to focus heavily on the potential of learning about probabilities, data analysis and statistics. These are the areas of maths that are inescapable in our modern lives.

Secondly, we need to change the way we see maths as a subject. Too often it's regarded as this separate subject that sits redundantly in the corner, while children learn equations from a textbook that they will never use. We need a syllabus that integrates statistics and data across every subject, as it is in our everyday lives. I want to see the potential of data wrangling demonstrated in History, or quantitative analysis of population growth in Geography. Or even how numbers can be used to create a visualisation in Art.

Finally, it's essential that we realise that being traumatised by maths is a genuine issue that a lot of people have experienced. Curing this phobia of the subject starts with teachers. With the right teacher, students can be inspired and pushed enough to achieve in maths, regardless of their natural ability. I believe you can make everybody feel comfortable with maths and the right teacher can make students fall in love with the subject, too.

This can only happen with an incredibly passionate and talented teaching force. But it is a very hard thing to do. Unless the Government invests in teachers who want to instil this love of the subject into students, Sunak's proposal is going to fall flat. All it will do is traumatise an entire new cohort of children. Without the proper support, forcing children to study maths until they are 18 will only make them hate the subject even more than they already do.

As told to Eleanor Peake.

5 January 2023

Children lost one-third of a year's learning to COVID, new study shows – but we need to think about the problem differently

An article from The Conversation.

By Clare Wood, Director, Centre for Research in Language, Education and Developmental Inequalities, Nottingham Trent University

Children's learning progress has slowed substantially during the pandemic, roughly equating to a loss of around 35% of the typical learning in a school year, according to a new study.

The analysis drew on 42 studies published between March 2020 and August 2022 from 15 different high- and middle-income countries (although most of the data was from the US, the UK and the Netherlands).

The researchers found that the learning deficits were higher in maths than in reading. They appeared early in the pandemic and remained stable, neither worsening over time (as some had feared) nor significantly improving.

So it appears that initiatives aimed at limiting the negative effects of school closures, such as online learning resources for home schooling, were successful in stabilising the initial impact of disruption to children's formal education.

At the same time, it would seem that we haven't yet found ways to support children to reach the levels of achievement we might have expected in normal circumstances. And this is particularly true for children from lower-income families.

A widening gap

This study confirms concerns expressed earlier in the pandemic by charities like the Sutton Trust that socioeconomic inequalities in learning progress would increase. For example, the shift to online learning during school closures created additional barriers for some children, where the availability of computers and internet access was not straightforward, or even impossible.

An analysis by the Education Policy Institute in 2017 found that at that time it would take the UK 50 years to close the attainment gap between pupils from disadvantaged backgrounds and their wealthier peers.

The National Foundation for Educational Research, a charity that conducts research into education and children's services, estimated that the effect of poverty on children's learning before the pandemic was at least twice as great as the impact of COVID's disruption to education.

However, it now seems clear that the gap has widened further, and is likely to take even longer to close.

Misplaced emphasis

But is this the right way to think about the challenges faced by schoolchildren and their teachers? The focus on 'lost learning' and the benchmarking of children's attainment to levels of pre-pandemic performance neglects an uncomfortable truth.

Many children have been fundamentally affected by the pandemic in other ways that will influence their ability to successfully learn, and which are not necessarily being addressed by the emphasis on 'catch up' learning.

For example, in November 2022 we published a white paper on the effects the pandemic has had on positivity, motivation to learn, resilience, and self-efficacy among children in key stage 2 (years 3–6).

Self-efficacy refers to a person's belief that they're capable of being successful in tasks or goals that they set for themselves. There is substantial evidence linking self-efficacy with academic achievement.

We found that while all four of these areas were negatively affected to some extent, it was children's sense of self-efficacy that was most strongly impacted. And although all areas have shown small signs of recovery, self-efficacy remains particularly low.

For the children in our research, self-efficacy referred to the belief that they could be successful not just with learning tasks, but also in terms of managing their emotions at school and their relationships with others in the classroom. The reduction in self-efficacy at school was apparent regardless of socioeconomic status.

So why might students' self-efficacy have suffered as a result of the pandemic? According to psychologist Albert Bandura, there are various ways in which we build our sense of self-efficacy. One is through direct experience of success in an environment that can facilitate this. This is what schools can do – they manage learning tasks to give children the experience of being successful.

A second way self-efficacy is built is via social comparison; by watching others like us being successful. This increases our sense that we can also succeed. The social isolation that children faced during lockdowns limited their ability to see other children like them engaging in learning and relate to their achievements.

Finally, an important avenue to self-efficacy is being with others who can reframe any negative reactions we might have to learning, such as failure or anxiety (for example, seeing nerves as a positive, and feeling excited about a new challenge rather than fear). Contact with teachers is important in helping children to reframe their feelings in these ways.

At home and at school

While it's important to recognise and document the academic toll that the pandemic has taken on children's learning, part of the reason our attempts to rectify things have been unsuccessful may be because we are failing to take into account the wider psychological effects that our children have experienced.

If we want to see children achieve, instead of discussions about 'learning loss' and 'falling behind', we need to focus some of our efforts on teaching them that they can have confidence in their abilities.

Teachers, and parents too, can do a lot to rebuild children's wellbeing and motivation to learn by addressing their basic psychological needs. This might include allowing them some control over what they do (autonomy), establishing a nurturing environment that the child feels connected to (relatedness), and enabling them to experience being successful (competence), perhaps by diversifying assessment methods.

30 January 2023

THE CONVERSATION

Most Britons say schools should provide school uniforms to families

By Joanna Morris, Data Journalist

Britons tend to support compulsory school uniforms

Most Britons believe children should wear uniforms to school – and nearly two-thirds say schools should help to provide them, according to a new YouGov Political Research survey.

Almost two thirds (65%) say that uniforms for secondary school pupils (children aged 11-16) should be compulsory, while 49% say they should be mandatory in primary schools (ages 4-11).

But the cost of clothing a child in full school uniform can run into hundreds of pounds every year, with added costs for every growth spurt along the way. Recent research by the Children's Society found the average yearly spend in 2020 was £337 for secondary school children and £315 for primary pupils.

In November 2021, the government introduced statutory guidance to help families cope with the cost by requiring branding - such as school logos - to be kept to a minimum, allowing parents to buy cheaper items from supermarkets and shops rather than school suppliers.

The guidance also stipulates that school websites should signpost parents to where second-hand uniforms are available and ensure uniform supplier arrangements are value for money.

Most Britons would like support to go further, with two-thirds (66%) saying schools should help to cover the cost of uniforms.

This includes more than a third of Brits (37%) who believe schools should help to meet the expense by providing uniforms to children from low-income homes, while an additional 29% say schools should give uniforms to all pupils.

Britons tend to back compulsory school uniforms

Do you think school uniforms for children should or should not be compulsory? %

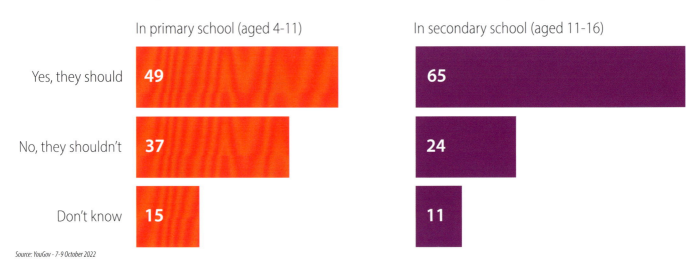

In primary school (aged 4-11)

Yes, they should	49
No, they shouldn't	37
Don't know	15

In secondary school (aged 11-16)

Yes, they should	65
No, they shouldn't	24
Don't know	11

Source: YouGov - 7-9 October 2022

Two-thirds of Britons think schools should help families cover uniform costs

Do you think school uniforms should or should not be provided by schools? %

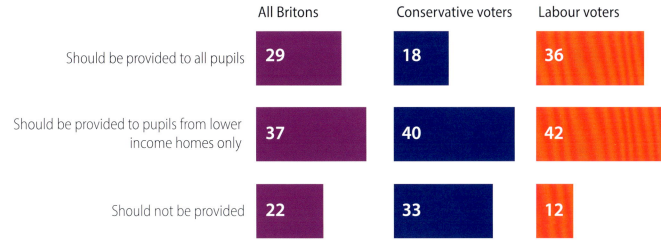

	All Britons	Conservative voters	Labour voters
Should be provided to all pupils	29	18	36
Should be provided to pupils from lower income homes only	37	40	42
Should not be provided	22	33	12

Source: YouGov - 7-9 October 2022

Britons closest to school age are less likely to want mandatory uniforms

Do you think school uniforms for children should or should not be compulsory? %

In primary schools

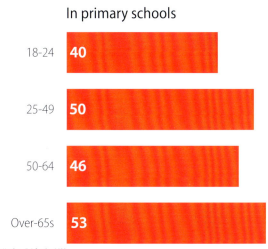

18-24	40
25-49	50
50-64	46
Over-65s	53

In secondary schools

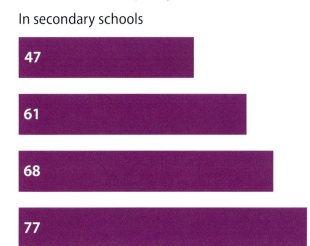

18-24	47
25-49	61
50-64	68
Over-65s	77

Source: YouGov - 7-9 October 2022

Only a fifth of the public (22%) think schools shouldn't have to contribute to the provision of uniforms at all.

Conservative voters are more opposed to schools paying towards uniforms, with 33% of those who voted Tory in the last general election saying so compared to 12% of Labour supporters.

At the same time, Tories are most likely to support the compulsory wearing of uniforms, with 81% saying they should be mandatory in secondary schools and 62% in primaries.

Labour voters still tend to support mandatory uniforms for children in secondary school (61% are in favour), although they are divided 42% to 46% on whether they should be required for children in primary school.

Older people are more likely to support compulsory uniforms

Those who left school decades ago are more likely to support school uniforms than those fresh out of education, though all age groups are more in favour of compulsory uniforms than against.

More than three-quarters of the over-65s (77%) say secondary uniforms should be compulsory, compared to fewer than half of those aged 18 to 24 (47% say they should be, 32% say they should not be).

And more than half of over-65s (53%) think they should be mandatory in primary schools, compared to 40% of 18 to 24-year-olds (34% say they should not be).

14 November 2022

Key Facts

- Most Britons believe children should wear uniforms to school – and nearly two-thirds say schools should help to provide them, according to a new YouGov Political Research survey.

- Recent research by the Children's Society found the average yearly spend in 2020 was £337 for secondary school children and £315 for primary pupils.

www.yougov.co.uk

Labour MPs call for universal free school meals for all primary school children

A growing number of Labour MPs are calling for Sadiq Khan's decision to provide free school meals for all primary school pupils in London to be rolled out across England.

By Nadine Batchelor-Hunt

The London mayor announced the year-long £130 million scheme on Monday, describing it as an emergency measure in response to the rising cost of living.

'The cost of living crisis means families and children across our city are in desperate need of additional support,' said Khan.

'I have repeatedly urged the government to provide free school meals to help already stretched families, but they have simply failed to act.'

He added: 'The difference they can make to children who are at risk of going hungry – and to families who are struggling to make ends meet – is truly game-changing.'

London has some of the highest rates of child poverty rates in the country – with 56% of children in Tower Hamlets below the poverty line, according to the Joseph Rowntree Foundation (JRF).

A number of Labour MPs have welcomed Khan's intervention, urging the government to implement the same policy nationwide.

Charlotte Nichols, MP for Warrington North, told PoliticsHome a 'universal approach' would enable pupils to fulfil their 'full academic potential'.

'This is something I would love to see rolled out across the UK, not only to end the stigma that sadly too often surrounds free school meals, but also as children can't learn if they're hungry and we have many children who are just missing out on this support, and whose parents are struggling to provide it,' said the Red Wall MP.

'A universal approach to free school meals would ensure all children can have quality, healthy, hot meals at school, and set them up for reaching their full academic potential.'

According to the JRF, 4.3m children in the UK live in poverty – with data from the Food Foundation in September 2022 revealing 4m children living in food insecurity in the UK.

Dawn Butler, MP for Brent Central and former shadow women and equalities secretary, told PoliticsHome universal school meals for primary school pupils was important for child development.

'I support and think that the sixth richest county should be able to ensure our children get at least one good meal a day as it will aid learning and development,' she said.

Nadia Whittome, MP for Nottingham East, encouraged the government to follow suit – warning there is 'no excuse for letting a single child go hungry' in the 'sixth richest country in the world'.

'The Mayor of London has the right idea – it's time for the Conservative government to follow suit,' she told PoliticsHome.

Former shadow chancellor John McDonnell also told PoliticsHome the move had his '100 per cent support'.

'Sadiq's announcement on free school meals is a huge breakthrough that will dramatically improve the lives of so many of our children in London and I am pressing for Labour to commit to this policy nationally,' he said.

'Preventing children going hungry at school is exactly what a Labour government should do and would have popular support.'

A coalition of charities – including Save The Children and Shelter – have warned that one in four UK homes are going without essentials amid the worsening cost of living crisis.

'Families are now existing month to month, even day to day in some cases and going without essentials, making us deeply worried about the impact this has on children,' said Dan Paskins, Director of UK Impact at Save The Children on Tuesday.

'The Spring Budget is a chance to take action to help families and one valuable step forwards would be to provide free school meals to all families on Universal Credit.'

A Downing Street spokesperson on Monday defended its record on the issue – but did not rule out future changes.

'Free school meal eligibility is under review, but we continue to believe it is important that it is targeted to ensure we are supporting those who need them most.'

21 February 2023

Making all schools into academies in the UK is wrong

By Kevin Courtney, General Secretary of the National Education Union, UK 6 April 2022

England's school system has undergone a radical transformation since 2010 with thousands of schools transferred into the control of private organisations called academy trusts. These are hybrid organisations – not-for-profit private trusts subject to company law which receive state funding but operate via a contract with central government, rather than a relationship with the local authority. Many different types of organisations have set up academy trusts, from large commercial companies, to churches, universities and wealthy private individuals.

Currently, around 80% of English secondary schools and nearly 40% of primary schools are academies. Although some trusts run 'stand-alone' academies, most academies are now in 'chains', known as Multi-Academy Trusts (MATs). The trend is towards consolidation into larger MATs, where a single trust board can be responsible for many schools – the largest MAT has more than 70 schools. A forthcoming government White Paper is likely to assert the government's wish for all schools in England to become academies within MATs.

This trend has fragmented the English school system, weakened and undermined democratically accountable local authorities, boosted the power of private actors, and increased scope for profiteering and commercial exploitation.

Where once there was a single local state employer, now many academy trusts can operate in one area. This has undermined local collective agreements and accelerated deregulation of school staff's terms and conditions, increasing the use of performance related pay. Average pay for teaching staff in academies is lower, but higher for senior management, with sky high salaries for some 'leaders' of academy trusts.

Academisation has also radically reduced the voice of local communities, parents and staff in the English school system. Once a school joins a MAT it cannot leave to return to the local authority or even choose another trust. Schools are absorbed into MATs, or are transferred between them, with no input from or even consultation of the communities they serve. Whereas local authority schools are required to have two elected parents on their boards of governors, there is no such requirement for academy trusts. Indeed, some MATs have even abolished their local governing bodies. Independent staff representation is also not required in MAT governance structures.

However, to understand the full impact of academisation, the policy should be seen as a fundamental part of a wider set of neoliberal education reforms which promote school choice, marketisation and competition as well as top-down forms of high stakes accountability.

Converting schools to academies, according to government dogma, is supposed to bring in the virtues of competition, choice and also – as its proponents see it – schools that are free from the restrictions and backwardness of the local state.

All this is supposed to boost results but even by this metric MATs have not succeeded: there is no evidence that academies outperform local authority schools. Echoing the same findings in the 2021/2 GEM Report on non-state actors at a global level, research by the Sutton Trust has found that two thirds of academy chains in the UK perform below average for disadvantaged pupils.

Meanwhile, academies are making the school system more centralised and top down – with a greater role for central government.

It is worth considering the results of a four-year study by academics from University College London (UCL) evaluating the impact of recent government reforms – encompassing academies and the operation of high stakes forms of accountability – which concluded that schools are more tightly regulated than ever, facing pressure to get good exam results and grades by Ofsted, the inspection authority, or face being taken over by a MAT.

Two-thirds of the 700 head teachers surveyed for the study agreed that inequalities between schools are becoming wider as a result of current government policy.

As the UCL study shows, this has very negative consequences for education staff. One aspect of this is the narrowing of the curriculum and 'scripted teaching': academy chains are often at the vanguard of promoting standardised teaching methodology and pupil assessment, which undermines teachers' professional autonomy and ability to employ their own pedagogical approaches.

Academies often have excessive accountability mechanisms in place – such as learning walks, book checks and constant teacher observations. These fuel excessive workloads, which are driving teachers out of the profession. They also undermine professional autonomy over teaching and learning.

Academies also undermine teacher professionalism as they can employ unqualified teachers. A 2019 study found academies were more likely than other schools with pupils from poorer backgrounds to hire more teachers without qualified teacher status.

Some academy chains have also adopted very strict and punitive behaviour policies which staff are expected to enforce. These policies have the dual effect of fuelling high levels of exclusions of those children who are classified as having special educational needs or who are seen as 'not fitting in', but also undermine more progressive pedagogical approaches to behaviour management.

As a trade union, the NEU is fighting back against the pernicious effects of the academies policy by empowering our members to take action when their school is being threatened with academisation. We also support members in academies to fight for and maintain better terms and conditions in academies, including the roll back of performance related pay.

An equitable system also needs to see the end of high stakes exams and the pressure of Ofsted. The NEU is campaigning for fundamental changes to the curriculum and assessment system. As part of this, the NEU has been working for the past year alongside academics, parents and students to support the Independent Assessment Commission, to build a new, fairer and more robust assessment and qualification system at secondary level.

While academies are an English phenomenon, it is important to see how the policy and its priorities connects to what is happening across the globe.

It is worth noting that Ark, a MAT of 39 schools in England, has an international arm that advises governments how to outsource management of public schools, for instance in Liberia and South Africa. This is mentioned in the 2021/2 GEM report and is also highlighted in the NEU's report In whose interest? The UK's role in privatising education around the world. The research shows that Ark has also been involved in advising the UK government on public-private partnerships through its Education Partnerships Group.

These connections show us that the drive to greater privatisation and marketisation in public education is a global movement. The NEU welcomes the spotlight shone on these trends by the GEM Report and will continue to advocate for public education to protect and promote equity and inclusion.

15 April 2022

Most schools to cut staff, axe repairs and up class sizes over funding crisis

Heads reveal 'catastrophic' and 'devastating' reality of rising costs.

By John Dickens

Most schools will likely cut staff, increase class sizes and axe building repairs over the coming years to deal with rising costs, with some secondaries facing a £500,000 hit.

A survey of 630 head teachers by the Association of School and College Leaders reveals the 'catastrophic' impact of the funding crisis on schools.

Nearly all schools (98 per cent) said they would have to make savings either this year or next to meet rising costs.

Inflation and soaring energy bills mean schools face a £2 billion shortfall by 2024, previous analysis suggests.

Two-thirds of schools are considering cutting support staff or scrapping or suspending capital projects. Over half say it is likely they will reduce staff and increase class sizes or reducing the number of teaching assistants.

Cost pressures include the unfunded teacher and support staff pay rises, rising catering costs and energy bills that one sector leader described as 'apocalyptic'.

Schools face costs equal to 10 teachers

Some secondary schools estimated the extra costs amounts to £500,000, the equivalent cost of employing 10 teachers.

Two in four schools were considering reducing their curriculum options, with music, drama and design and technology most likely for the axe.

One head described the situation as 'Devastating. I have been here for 15 years and put my heart and soul into improving this school. It has been tough, but it has worked; this is now going to be thrown away.'

Another said it was 'Catastrophic. The scale of savings required in-year is unachievable.

'Our forecast budget, which was previously positive, is now dire. We would have to fundamentally change our offer to manage. The quality of education we will be able to provide will be substantially reduced.'

Seventeen schools (2.7 per cent) said they are considering a four-day week.

Local authority-maintained schools are required to run at least two sessions on every school day, but there is no such rules for academies.

Geoff Barton, ASCL general secretary, said the 'future is bleak unless the government acts urgently.

'No government can claim to be serving the public interest by presiding over an education funding crisis which cuts provision and imperils standards. And no government which does so can expect to remain in power at the next General Election.'

New prime minister Rishi Sunak warned that 'difficult decision' will be needed to find public spending cuts.

But Barton said it should be clear 'it is simply untenable to once again sacrifice schools and colleges on the altar of austerity, as happened in the wake of the last financial crisis.

Education must not be 'soft target for government cuts'

'Education should not be seen as a soft target for government cuts but a vital public service and an investment in the future.'

More than nine in ten schools that answered a recent survey by school leaders' union NAHT said they will be in deficit next year unless they make 'significant cuts'.

It is simply untenable to once again sacrifice schools and colleges on the altar of austerity

Union deputy general secretary Nick Brook called on new education secretary Gillian Keegan to 'urgently get to grips with the reality of the situation … and make a compelling case to the Treasury for the funding so urgently needed'.

Schools Week revealed last week that some councils have as many as half their schools in deficit. Meanwhile more than 350 academy trusts recently signed a letter expressing 'grave concerns' over the funding squeeze on the 'viability' of their schools.

A Department for Education spokesperson said they 'understand that schools are facing cost pressures'. This is why schools core funding has risen by £4 billion this year.

The six-month energy guarantee scheme will also provide 'greater certainty over their budgets over the winter months.

'We are also providing schools with tools and information to help get the best value for money from their resources.'

27 October 2022

The school starting age

An extract from *Class Rules: the truth about Scottish schools* by James McEnaney.

By James McEnaney

In recent years one fairly radical idea – at least for Scotland – has attracted increasing levels of attention and widespread support: changing the age at which pupils start school. Right now, children in Scotland start primary school at either four or five – but many believe that this should not happen until the age of seven.

Although we naturally assume that our traditional approach represents good sense and normality, the truth is actually quite different. Across the world, fewer than 15% of countries send their children to school aged four or five, and almost all of them have direct historical links to the uk through the British Empire. The overwhelming majority of countries actually send their children to school aged six, a full two years later than some children in Scotland head off to primary school, and there are more countries with a starting age of seven than there are those adopting the approach we simply take for granted.

What's more, there seems to be little rationale for our unusually young starting age beyond the fact that things have always been this way. If we were starting to build a public school system from scratch, how many of us would be arguing that the best place for a four-year-old child is a school classroom, or that they should be spending their time pursuing academic benchmarks rather than playing with their friends? Indeed, there are some very real concerns about the impact of sending children to school at such an early stage, with critics of the status quo citing the damage that can be done to young people's emotional and mental health when we try to force them through a system for which they simply are not ready. You can't force a caterpillar to turn into a butterfly and you risk doing a lot of damage if you try.

Those opposing change would perhaps argue that these concerns are outweighed by the outright educational advantages experienced by children in the UK – since they go to school earlier than their peers in other nations, they must also learn more and consequently outperform them? Not so. In 'top performing' countries such as Estonia, Canada and Finland schooling starts at six or seven years old. In New Zealand, parents can wait until their child's sixth birthday before sending them to primary school, a stark contrast to Scotland's approach where children begin school at the start of a pre-determined academic year. A 2009 review of Pisa data found no evidence that starting school earlier led to increased reading levels by the age of 15.

Those pushing for change, such as backers of the Upstart Scotland campaign, argue that children benefit most from a play-based experience that aids their overall development, not a system that values measurable reading, writing and counting skills above all else. They also believe that a kindergarten system would help to ensure that all children benefit from play-based, pupil-focused learning, avoiding the current postcode lottery where some schools have adopted varying degrees of this approach (typically for their youngest pupils) while others have not.

One central principle behind implementing a play-based, ringfenced kindergarten stage across the entire country is that it would protect children from the harms that can be done by a system that prioritises data and deadlines over wellbeing. Another is to help restore opportunities for active, social, outdoor play that are so crucial to children's all-round development. It's not that a kindergarten stage would, for example, mean that children would not learn to read until they start primary school at seven years old, simply that they would not be pushed to do so before they are ready in order to meet one-size-fits-all performance targets and curricular benchmarks. As any parent knows, during those early years children develop at markedly different rates and in entirely different ways: the one constant is that play and inquiry are how they learn. There is little if anything to be gained from ignoring these entirely natural variations, but there is increasing evidence that doing so can be damaging to young people's lifelong learning and wellbeing.

Like many people across Scotland, I have been convinced that raising the school starting age, combined with a revolutionary investment in developing a universal kindergarten system, is probably the ideal starting point for improving Scottish schooling – but the second part of that proposition is crucial.

If we want to do something about the injustices that manifest in the earliest stages of children's lives we should start, as the song says, at the very beginning, but simply sending children to school a couple of years later, while leaving the rest of our systems and approaches largely unchanged, would likely serve only to widen the divides between the richest and poorest families. By the time children reach two and a half years old, measurable gaps between rich and poor have already appeared. One of the Scottish Government's own 'attainment gap' measures shows that more than 70% of children from the most affluent areas show 'no concerns' at their 27–30 month review, but that the figure for those from the most deprived areas is just 55%. More broadly, there is widespread evidence of massive vocabulary gaps between children from different social backgrounds by the time they are even toddlers, a divide that is driven by different early life experiences as opposed to innately different ability levels.

Sending children to school too early is only likely to exacerbate, rather than ameliorate, these issues. The development of a national kindergarten system, universally available to all children from the ages of three to seven, with mixed-aged groupings, and either massively subsidised by or entirely paid for through general taxation (just like primary and secondary school), would help to focus attention and resources on the vitally important early years. It is one of the very few policy changes that could begin to equalise the foundational experiences of children across Scotland and taking such a step could be just the catalyst we need to rethink not just the school system but also some of our fundamental social assumptions.

Success would depend on both expertise and infrastructure. We would need to see the development of a well-qualified and high-status workforce and the construction of appropriate physical spaces (combining new or converted buildings with outdoor learning environments) across the country. In the end, the goal should be the creation of a truly national early years sector to replace the current patchwork of provision that further entrenches the divide between rich and poor. All of this would cost money, although given that we currently educate children from four years old anyway and are in the process of a significant expansion in early years provision, a lot of the resources are already likely to be in place.

This sort of change might also raise questions about the overall structures of primary and secondary schooling in Scotland. Just like with the school starting age, there is a tendency to believe that our current approach is also the ideal one, but what if we're wrong? If we were to raise the starting age of formal schooling from four or five to seven, would it then make sense to reassess the point at which children shift from primary school to secondary? Should we perhaps go further, and ask whether the introduction of a middle stage – such as those used in countries like the usa, Japan or Norway – might be more compatible with cfe and allow us to better meet the needs of young people? Maybe it would be better to alter our approach to the final years of high school so that those aged 16–18 learn in an environment that looks and functions much more like a college, thus ensuring that they are better prepared to take their next steps after leaving the school system?

There's really no reason why all of this shouldn't be up for debate, even if it means overcoming the small-c conservatism that so often dominates our approach to education. Sometimes it is worth asking how much of the status quo would be replicated if we were building a system from scratch and then using the answer to help us focus on the possibilities for progress rather than the limits of the present.

The biggest barrier to these sorts of structural changes is probably political. Although some aspects of early learning could be improved relatively quickly, especially given the recent publication of updated guidance for early years education in Scotland, there is absolutely no way that the entire landscape of Scottish education could be redesigned and rebuilt within a five-year window. These are generational changes for which no single government is going to be able to claim the credit, so why start the process at all? It is also worth bearing in mind that the chaos and anger sparked by endless, aimless animosity over schools suits some politicians just fine. Keeping people outraged is, after all, a more effective way of shoring up your vote (and keeping your job) than cross-chamber collaboration.

Changes on the sort of scale we require would demand the construction of a broad, forward-thinking, long-term consensus – to be blunt, it isn't clear that our elected representatives are up to that job. Perhaps they can surprise us.

27 September 2022

Four major challenges facing Britain's education system after the pandemic

An article from The Conversation.

By Helena Gillespie, University of East Anglia

The UK goverment's Department for Education has some new ministers in charge following the political turmoil surrounding Boris Johnson's resignation. After resigning only two days into the job of education secretary, Michelle Donelan has been replaced by James Cleverly, MP for Braintree.

Donelan's former role overseeing higher education has been filled by Andrea Jenkyns, MP for Morley and Outwood, who has been named skills, further and higher education minister. Jenkyns' credentials as an educational leader were called somewhat into question when she was photographed making a gesture to the public gathered outside Downing Street that would certainly have landed her in detention.

While these appointments can be considered, to some extent, to be caretaker roles pending the appointment of the new prime minister in early September, the new ministers still face significant challenges as they oversee schools, colleges and universities. Here are four issues facing them as they get to work.

Getting exams back to normal

The first hurdle comes next month with the annual round of GCSE and A-level exam results. This will be the first cohort since 2019 to have formally sat their exams. The Department for Education will be hoping that the exam results, which have already been taken and marked, will not cause such headline grabbing disruption this summer as in the two previous years.

In 2020, the first year that exams were cancelled due to the pandemic, results were overturned after it became clear that the algorithm used by the government to standardise grades was penalising students from disadvantaged backgrounds. Pupils could choose to use teacher assessments to decide grades instead.

In 2021, the government again elected to use teacher assessment to decide results, but the approach resulted in many more top grades. The jump in A grades at A-level, from 38% to 44%, meant that there were not enough places at top universities to go around – and universities had to offer prospective students packages of support to persuade them to defer to a 2022 start.

However, it is likely that the return to exams will mean a drop in grades from 2021, and there may be many disappointed students and parents. Weathering grade fluctuations in future years while also closing gaps in attainment for students from disadvantaged backgrounds will be a difficult trick to pull off.

Addressing inequality

In November 2020, the Department for Education launched its flagship initiative to address pandemic learning loss in England, the National Tutoring Programme – which pairs schools with tutors who work with individual students or small groups to help them catch up in core subjects.

However, the House of Commons Education Committee recently reported that the National Tutoring Programme is

failing to make an impact in the schools in deprived areas where children are most behind with their education.

Problems with the catch-up strategy are just the tip of the iceberg when it comes to endemic inequalities in education in the UK. School buildings in many areas are facing pressure from growing class sizes and wear and tear. A 2021 report by the Department for Education put the backlog of school maintenance in England at a cost of £11.4 billion, an eye watering sum at a time of economic crisis.

It is difficult to see how schools can level up for their pupils in buildings that are falling down. The education secretary must hope for sympathy and support around the new cabinet table to access the funds needed.

Provide support for teachers

The pandemic has had a serious impact on children and young people's mental health and wellbeing and the problem remains acute. One of the short-term impacts of this is growing pressures on teachers in classrooms. For this reason as well as the rise in the cost of living, teachers are asking for a substantial pay increase.

It seems unlikely that current proposals for pay rises in schools, which sit below the rate of inflation, will stop a ballot on strike action or address teacher shortages caused by so many leaving the profession. If the new minister is to be able to deliver meaningful educational recovery, schools are going to need to be better staffed and better supported by other sector agencies. Achieving this looks both difficult and expensive.

Free speech in higher education

On 27 June 2022, before her promotion to education secretary and subsequent resignation, Michelle Donelan had written to university vice chancellors advising them to consider whether their membership of certain diversity schemes was appropriate given their responsibility to uphold free speech. This was regarded with concern by many in the education sector as a move that blurred the lines between appropriate regulation and university autonomy.

In addition, the controversial Higher Education (Freedom of Speech) Bill, which seeks to ensure that free speech is protected on campus by limiting the 'no-platforming' of speakers, is currently passing through the House of Lords. However, a recent survey has found that 61% of students think that universities should prioritise protecting students from discrimination rather than permitting unlimited free speech.

The new Department for Education team has much to do to ensure that good decisions are made on behalf of the UK's children and young people.

19 July 2022

Useful Websites

Useful Websites

www.bellacaledonia.org.uk

www.educationhub.blog.gov.uk

www.ifs.org.uk

www.independent.co.uk

www.inews.co.uk

www.openaccessgovernment.org

www.politicshome.com

www.schoolsweek.co.uk

ww.shoutoutuk.org

www.telegraph.co.uk

www.theconversation.com

www.theguardian.com

www.ukeducation.info

www.world-education-blog.org

www.yougov.co.uk

Academy

Academies (under the Academies Bill 2010) are schools that are state-maintained, but independently run and funded by external sponsors. This gives the school greater freedom from local authority bureaucracy: for example how much they pay their staff and the subjects students are taught. Often, failing state schools are encouraged to apply for academy status.

A-levels

These are qualifications usually taken by students aged 16 to 18 at schools and sixth-form colleges, although they can be taken at any time by school leavers at local colleges or through distance learning. They provide an accepted route to degree courses and university and usually take two years to complete.

Comprehensive school

Also known as state schools, comprehensive schools are the state-run, Government-funded schools in Britain. Education is free in comprehensive schools.

Faith school

A faith school is subject to the national curriculum, but is affiliated to a particular religious faith or denomination.

Free school

Free schools have the same freedoms and flexibilities as academies, but they do not normally replace an existing school. Free schools may be set up by a wide range of proposers – including charities, universities, businesses, educational groups, teachers and groups of parents.

Further education

Education for 16- to 18-years-olds, for example college or sixth form.

GCSE

This stands for General Certificate of Secondary Education; it is the national exam taken by 16-year-olds in England and Wales. The Scottish equivalent is the Scottish Certificate of Education.

Grammar school

Grammar schools are state secondary schools in England that select their pupils by ability. The examination taken to enter a grammar school is known as the 11-plus. Grammar schools in Wales and Scotland are non-selective.

IGCSE

Introduced in 1988, International GCSE is an alternative to the traditional GCSEs, offered by Cambridge and Edexcel exam boards.

International Baccaluareate (IB or IBac)

An alternative to A-levels, the IBac was developed in Switzerland and is highly regarded by Universities.

Multi Academy Trusts (MATs)

A multi-academy trust (MAT) is a group of aligned educational academies that come together to form a trust. While local authority schools are required to have two elected parents on their boards of governors, there is no such requirement for academy trusts

National curriculum

The statutory set of guidelines set down by the Government which determines the subject material and attainment targets taught in schools in England and Wales. The National Curriculum applies to pupils up to the age of 16.

Private school

Sometimes known as 'public school', a private school is an independent, privately run school which charges fees to attend instead of being funded by the Government. Many private schools in the UK have charitable status, which means they are able to take advantage of various tax concessions such as being exempt from VAT. Also, pupils do not have to follow the national curriculum.

SATs

End of Key Stage Tests and Assessments (more commonly known as SATs) are national tests that children take twice during their primary school life. First, at the end of Key Stage 1 (KS1) in Year 2, and then second at the end of Key Stage 2 (KS2) in Year 6.

Sixth Form

Sixth form is a type of post-16 education which enables students to study for their A-levels or equivalents. Some sixth-form institutions are independent colleges, whilst others are attached to secondary schools.

State school

A school which is funded and run by the Government, at no cost to the pupils. An independent school, on the other hand, is one which is privately run and which pupils pay a fee to attend. These are sometimes known as 'private schools' or 'public schools' (please note, not all private schools are public schools).

T Levels

Launched in September 2020, T Levels are 2-year courses which are taken after GCSEs and are broadly equivalent to 3 A Levels. T Levels offer students practical and knowledge-based learning preparing them for apprenticeships, entry to skilled employment or related technical studies in higher education.

Vocational learning

Education that provides practical training for a specific occupation or vocation, for example agriculture, carpentry or beauty therapy. Traditionally this is delivered through 'hands-on' experience rather than academic learning, although there may be a combination of these elements depending on the course.

Index

A

academies 1–3, 35–36, 43

age, starting school 38–39

A-levels 4–5, 7, 11, 14–16, 40, 43

alternative provision 3

arts subjects 17–19

assessments 11

attainment gaps 22–24

B

baccalaureate *see* British baccalaureate; international baccalaureate (IB)

boarding schools 1

British baccalaureate 4–5

BTecs 15–16

C

city technology colleges 1

comprehensive schools *see* state-funded schools

COVID-19 pandemic, impact on education 6, 30–31, 40–41

E

education

    challenges to 40–41

    competition in 11

    funding 6–10

    inequality in 22–24, 40–41

    reforms 4–5

    statistics 6–7

    see also schools

employment 6–7

F

faith schools 1, 43

family background 24

family life 25

free school meals 22–23, 34

free schools 1, 3, 43

free speech 41

further education (FE) 6, 43

G

GCSEs 4, 11, 23–24, 40

grammar schools 26–28, 43

H

higher education (HE) 16, 41

    see also university

home schooling 1

I

independent schools 1, 11

inequality 22–24, 40–41

international baccalaureate (IB) 12–13, 43

international GCSEs 43

M

mathematics 4–5, 29

mental health 25

multi-academy trusts (MATs) 2, 35–36, 43

N

National Curriculum 1

NEET (not in education, employment or training) 6–7

O

Ofsted (Office for Standards in Education, Child Services and Skills) 1,2

P

population boom 7–8

poverty 22–24

private schools 26–28, 43

provision, alternative 3

    see also schools

Q

qualifications 4–5, 7, 15–16

R

rules 20–21

S

SATs (End of Key Stage Tests and Assessments) 43

schools

    starting age 38–39

    state v private 26–28

    types of 1–3

    see also education; types of school by name

school uniforms 32–33

self-efficacy 31

self-esteem 25

SHAPE subjects 17–19

sixth form 6, 11, 43

socio-economic status 24

special educational needs or disabilities (SEND) pupils 3

special schools 1

state-funded schools 1–2, 26–28, 43

STEM (science, technology, engineering and maths) 17–19

strict schools 20–21

studio schools 1

T

teachers

    recruitment 4–5

    support for 41

T-levels 4, 7, 15–16, 43

training 6–7

U

uniforms 32–33

university 11, 14

university technical colleges 1

V

vocational learning 43

vocational qualifications 15–16

W

wellbeing 25